LEADING AT THE SPEED OF CHANGE

LEADING AT THE SPEED OF CHANGE

USING NEW ECONOMY RULES TO INVIGORATE OLD ECONOMY COMPANIES

BILL CAPODAGLI
LYNN JACKSON

McGraw-Hill

New York   Chicago   San Francisco   Lisbon   London   Madrid
Mexico City   Milan   New Delhi   San Juan   Seoul
Singapore   Sydney   Toronto

Library of Congress Cataloging-in-Publication Data
Capodagli, Bill.
  Leading at the speed of change : using new economy rules to invigorate
old economy companies / Bill Capodagli, Lynn Jackson.
    p.   cm.
  Includes bibliographical references and index.
  ISBN 0-07-137079-X
  1. Strategic alliances (Business)   2. Teams in the workplace.   3. Leadership.
4. Organizational change.   5. Business enterprises—Technological innovations.
I. Jackson, Lynn.   II. Title.
HD69.S8 C36 2001
658.4'06   2001030255

McGraw-Hill

*A Division of The **McGraw·Hill** Companies*

JK

1 2 3 4 5 6 7 8 9 0   AGM/AGM   0 9 8 7 6 5 4 3 2 1

ISBN 0-07-137079-X

This book was set in Janson by McGraw-Hill's Professional Book Group composition
unit, Hightstown, NJ.

Printed and bound by Quebecor World/Martinsburg.

To all those in the world of business who—

Dream of transforming their cultures,

Believe in the entrepreneurial spirit,

Dare to reinvent old ways of doing business, and

Do all it takes to serve the customer and strive together to make the Dream a reality!

Contents

Part IV

Do

Foreword

In less than a decade, the Internet economy has surpassed century-old industries such as telecommunications, airlines, and utilities in terms of revenues. Milestones that took up to 100 years to achieve in the Industrial Age are occurring at a staggering pace in this new economy. This type of unprecedented growth underscores the strategic role and impact of the Internet, and indicates that companies and countries realize that the Internet is key to their future success and survival.

The rise of the Internet economy can be tied to a new business model in which companies work together to create value for their joint customers. For example, in the 1980s, leading companies focused on internal development to create competitive advantage. In the 1990s, successful companies relied on both internal development and acquisitions.

This decade, leading companies will be those that develop internally, acquire effectively, and form ecosystem partnerships in a horizontal business model. Unlike a vertical business model, in which a single company attempts to excel in every aspect of the business, the horizontal model allows multiple companies to combine their expertise to create comprehensive solutions for their customers.

As a result, big and small companies around the globe are competing on a level playing field. Borders around and boundaries between countries are dissolving, creating a 24/7 marketplace.

The companies that will survive and thrive in this new economy will be those that harness the power of partnerships to turn this fast pace of change into competitive advantage. For example, Cisco and AT&T Solutions are committed to creating Internet solutions that will empower customers with the agility, speed, and technology to differentiate themselves from their competition.

Cisco and AT&T have been working together since 1996 and are equally committed to creating a win-win partnership for our customers, our shareholders, and our employees. Our relationship has been defined through a number of challenges and opportunities, and we have both benefited from our joint efforts.

Leading at the Speed of Change outlines how AT&T Solutions has evolved its organization to meet the changing demands and opportunities of today's fast-paced Internet economy. Readers will also gain insight into how a leading company such as AT&T has evolved its business model and strategy to position itself for success in the coming decade.

John Chambers
President and CEO
Cisco Systems

Preface

I t's unusual to be having a child at the age of 110, but on February 14, 1995, that's just what AT&T did. On that date, AT&T Solutions came into the world, and the network outsourcing world hasn't been the same since.

Conceived in an AT&T conference room by a maverick 12-person visionary group, AT&T Solutions was precocious from birth. As an outsourcing consultant, it offered IT networking services to companies desperate to survive in the new economy, but unable to keep up with the fast-evolving technology and overwhelmed by the task of making it all work. By designing and managing their networks for them, AT&T Solutions enabled these companies to focus on their core businesses instead.

And thus, in just five years, AT&T Solutions became a gigantic success.

How did this happen? How did a high-speed enterprise launch itself from within a classically lumbering corporate organization such as AT&T? How did it confound the naysayers' doubts? How did it beat the catch-22 of winning its first clients without a track record of proven success?

And how, once it could walk, did it learn to run at the speed of change? How have its strategic alliances, its team-focused approach, and, most significantly, its culture of vision, courage, and integrity kept it aloft?

And will high-flying AT&T Solutions ever succumb to corporate entropy, and fall back to earth?

What role can AT&T Solutions play in the new economy?

These are some of the questions examined in this book.

Leading at the Speed of Change is the story of a phenomenal business success, but it's not your typical start-up, sellout, take-the-money-and-run tale of whiz kids on the make. It's an absorbing and instructive account of entrepreneurial vision, perseverance, and guts.

Walt Disney said, "I dream, I test my dreams against my beliefs, I dare to take risks, and I execute my vision to make those dreams come true."[1]

DREAM. BELIEVE. DARE. DO.

These actions speak louder than words—and are given pitch, volume, and purpose by the value-creating ideals that thread through this book:

Vision
Values
Alliances
Acculturation
Customer intimacy
Predictable problems
Failing forward fast
Quintessential teams

Just as the Dream, Believe, Dare, Do principles galvanized Walt Disney's business-as-show-business approach, so they did for the AT&T Solutions team.

Our story demonstrates—by AT&T Solutions' highly acclaimed "good show" performance along with our own prescriptive advice—how this formula can do the same for you.

We've based our consulting practice, Capodagli Jackson Consulting, and all of our books on our *Dream*ovations model. *Dream*ovations is a holistic strategy to build a company using Disney's guiding principles Dream, Believe, Dare, Do and reflects a business-as-show-business approach.

AT&T Solutions' success is proof that business-as-show-business does not only apply to the entertainment field. Indeed, today's brightly lit, globalized new economy is transforming business into the greatest show on earth.

Bill Capodagli
Lynn Jackson

Acknowledgments

If new-economy success is all about the ability to continuously create and to self-transform fast, then AT&T Solutions has surely arrived. Never looking tired or out of date, they close one chapter and almost overnight begin writing a new one that affirms their drive to dream, believe, dare, and do, all at the speed of change. Out with old structures, antiquated physical operations, and competition based on price alone. This is the story of how AT&T Solutions met every one of these challenges and more in positioning itself as a new icon in the Internet economy of today.

The people at AT&T, AT&T Solutions, and their clients and partners who have helped us bring this phenomenal cultural drama to life surely compose the upper strata of leadership. They are running at speeds almost unheard of in the last millennium, as evidenced by their energized visions, intellects, and attitudes, which allow them to compete and win.

Here are the headliners and legends of *Leading at the Speed of Change*:

MaryAnn Sweeney from McGraw-Hill, who believed that the AT&T Solutions message would challenge leaders to allow the entrepreneurial spirit to soar, moving their organizations to new heights.

Rick Roscitt, the protagonist, who reminds us that no management model can anticipate and predict everything that may happen—that you must play it out and believe in the power of a culture that makes everything work.

Brian Maloney, President of AT&T Solutions, who empowers the AT&T Solutions culture to execute and grow by putting people, both the AT&T Solutions staff and the client, first.

Mike Armstrong, CEO of AT&T, the man at the top whose leadership understands that it's the fast—not just the big—who prevail.

John Chambers, CEO of Cisco Systems, role model extraordinaire for partnering in the new economy.

Frank Ianna, President of AT&T Network Services, whose foresight created the new face of networking services, blending high-tech with high-touch.

Mary Ellen Caro, Vice President and COO of AT&T Data Internet Services, whose passion for the AT&T Solutions idea continues to inspire team members.

Bill O'Brien, Vice President of Marketing of AT&T Solutions, who echoes what clients really want in the new economy: specific, and personal, solutions, not those of old corporate America.

We sincerely thank the following people for their time, candor, and total dedication to this process throughout our countless hours of interviews:

Marv Adams, CTO, Bank One

Joseph Alutto, Dean, Fisher College of Business, The Ohio State University

Dick Anderson, CTO, AT&T Solutions

Bill Blinn, VP Human Resources, AT&T Solutions

Ken Bohlen, Senior VP and CIO, Textron

Lynn Brown, HR Manager Outsourcing Practice, AT&T Solutions

Jim Byrnes, Public Relations, AT&T Solutions

Dr. Quiester Craig, Dean, School of Business & Economics, North Carolina A&T State University

John Damian, Managing Partner Service Delivery, AT&T Solutions

Dawn DiMartino, Marketing Communications Director, AT&T Solutions

Bill Etherington, Senior VP and Group Executive, Sales & Distribution, IBM Global Services

Russ Fairchild, AT&T Solutions' Engagement General Manager, Chase Manhattan

Bill Gauld, CIO, Sony

Bob Heinz, GCSC Client Engagement Manager, AT&T Solutions

Bob Hilkin, AT&T Solutions' Engagement Team Member, Textron

Tom Hogan, University Relations, AT&T Business Services

Mike Keller, Senior Vice President of Business & Partner Management for IT, Bank One

Sal Lipari, AT&T Solutions' Engagement General Manager, Merrill Lynch

Dr. Nino Masnari, Dean, College of Engineering, North Carolina State University

Denis O'Leary, Executive Vice President, Chase Manhattan

Patrick O'Malley, Managing Partner, AT&T Solutions

Gerry Pape, AT&T Solutions' Engagement General Manager, IBM

Scott Perry, VP Strategic Alliances, AT&T Solutions

Bob Scheier, Managing Partner Business Development, AT&T Solutions

Howard Shallcross, former CIO, Merrill Lynch

Dr. Dan Short, Dean, Richard T. Farmer School of Business, Miami University

John Skubik, Executive Vice President, Bank One

Glenn Swift, AT&T Solutions' Engagement General Manager, Bank One

Rob Vatter, AT&T Solutions' Engagement General Manager, Textron

Greg Walters, Director of Organizational & Professional Development, AT&T Solutions

Doug Williams, former CIO, Chase Manhattan

John Wood, Vice President and Managing Partner, New Client Engagements, AT&T Solutions

We would also like to thank the many members of both AT&T Solutions and their client teams for their insights.

A special thank you to Susan Caswell of AT&T Solutions, who coordinated our entire interview schedule in multiple cities and provided invaluable support at every turn.

Thank you to Kate Wehmeyer of AT&T Solutions for her invaluable help.

Thanks to Audra Kieffaber and Pete Fairfield at Capodagli Jackson Consulting, who now truly understand the words *at the speed of change*.

A big thanks to Cassandra Smiley, our creative graphics artist, whose visual imagery adds clarity and depth to the words.

A heartfelt thank you to our editor, Peter Maeck, who asks the right questions and brings definition to all the facets of Dream, Believe, Dare, and Do within the AT&T Solutions story.

And many thanks to Mary Glenn, who did a fabulous job of helping us balance all the variables of this dynamic process.

LEADING
AT THE
SPEED OF
CHANGE

Introduction

In February 1993, Rick Roscitt ha d a dream. Not at night while he was sleeping, but with his eyes open wide. He imagined a press story like this one:

COMMUNICATIONS WEEK

FEBRUARY 20, 1995

AT&T LAUNCHES OUTSOURCING UNIT

AT&T launched a network management and outsourcing business unit last week, offering large customers one-stop shopping for end-to-end network design, installation, and operation.

The unit, called AT&T Solutions, incorporates AT&T's existing network management services, communications services, and products from AT&T's network services and computer divisions, as well as new consulting systems integration services.

"What's new about AT&T Solutions is that it's totally focused on providing network-based integrated solutions for our customers," said Richard Roscitt, vice president and general manager of the new unit.

Then Rick saw headlines of subsequent years proclaiming successive triumphs in an unfolding blockbuster tale …

FOR RELEASE TUESDAY, APRIL 9, 1996
  MASTERCARD INTERNATIONAL AWARDS NETWORK
  OUTSOURCING CONTRACT TO AT&T SOLUTIONS

FOR RELEASE TUESDAY, MARCH 10, 1998
  CITIBANK CHOOSES AT&T SOLUTIONS
  TO MANAGE GLOBAL DATA NETWORKS

FOR RELEASE THURSDAY, JANUARY 13, 2000
  ACER AWARDS MULTI-YEAR CONTRACT
  FOR GLOBAL NETWORKING TO AT&T SOLUTIONS

In 1993 Roscitt was a 21-year veteran at AT&T, having arrived in 1972 with a B.E. from Stevens Institute of Technology and an MBA from the Sloan School of Management at MIT.

When he first came to AT&T, his father, grandfather, uncles, and brothers were not too happy with his choice. All of them were proud, independent business owners, and they warned Rick against becoming just a cog in a giant corporate machine.

"They told me big companies are dogmatic and slow and stodgy and don't like people breaking ranks," recalls Rick. "But I was afraid of taking my big ambitions to a small company that wouldn't have the courage or the money to support them. A big company would at least have the money."

At AT&T Rick gained a reputation for being outspoken and a bit of a renegade. "I never got appraised as the best guy in the group," he says, "because they couldn't stomach the idea of making me the role model. It didn't matter what the results were."

"You're dead," said a longtime AT&T executive to Rick one day.

"What do you mean?" said Rick.

The executive, who was about to retire after 30 years' service, explained: "The corporate body treats new things like foreign substances and tries to expel them. If you're the new thing, you're out."

"What if the new thing brings value to the organization?" Rick asked him.

"Big corporations," the executive chuckled, "eat their young."

Rick mulled this for a while. "And then somewhere along the line," he recalls, "I just accepted it and said to the company, 'I'm going to be who I am, you be who you are, and we'll see if we can coexist.'"

They coexisted just fine, it turned out, with Rick leading the engineering, installation, and operation of AT&T's long-distance network in the central United States. He then became vice president of the company's Outbound Business Services, which launched the highly successful "We Want You Back" advertising campaign that won an Effie Award for advertising excellence. After that, he managed the largest-ever national conversion from analog to digital switching systems.

And now here he was in early 1993, dreaming of plunging AT&T into information technology (IT) outsourcing—though the company had no outsourcing business plan and no significant network outsourcing experience.

Only a maverick would dream a dream like that.

He was seriously considering taking on Chase Manhattan Bank as a first client—while his boss was away on vacation!

Only a renegade would do that.

Or a nut.

Why didn't Rick wait to consult his boss before making this commitment? What was his big rush?

"We'd set up Chase's telecommunications network," Rick explains. "They'd been running it themselves, but it had gotten too complex and now they needed help. They wanted us to manage it as an outsourcer. Well, we thought about it for three months, and then they came to us and laid it on the line. They said, 'We think you are the right ones to do it. You have the whole network now, you have more skill than we have, and you wrote the book on network management. Will you do it?'"

Rick said yes.

"My boss was mad as hell when he came back," he recalls. "He said we were entering into an arrangement we didn't understand, and that we didn't know what the hell we were doing because we'd never written or managed an outsourcing contract. We were making commitments beyond what we could assuredly achieve. And you know what? He was right!"

Well, not totally right. Although Rick's commitment was a leap of faith, it couldn't be said that the faith was unjustified.

"After we went ahead with Chase," recounts Rick, "we noticed that a number of companies were bundling the outsourcing of their networks to general purpose outsourcers like EDS and CSC. We looked at those relationships, and we researched computer data center outsourcing, which at this point had been going on for about 10 years. We examined the Andersen Consulting model, interviewed prospective customers, and checked out every RFP [request for proposal] that appeared. We studied all of this pretty hard, and we realized there was something big happening here, bigger than we thought. It looked like an opportunity we just had to pursue."

But hadn't Rick heard that big corporations eat their young?

Would that warning come true? Of course it would, as soon as the Chase arrangement flopped.

But it didn't flop; it thrived.

And Rick kept dreaming. And investigating. And making the rounds within AT&T for support. And one day his original dream—of launching a unit dedicated to network outsourcing—came true.

"In the beginning," says Rick, "we were so small that nobody paid attention to us. We didn't get a lot of respect from the rest of AT&T because we were nothing. We were pretty much an orphan or stepchild off to the side."

Could this orphan survive? Most likely not, it seemed at the time. The obituary was probably already written.

But when the next day came and went, the orphan's heart was still beating. And it got stronger with each day, month, and year:

FOR RELEASE TUESDAY, MAY 7, 1996
AT&T SOLUTIONS SUPPORTS MERRILL LYNCH VISION
WITH ELECTRONIC COMMERCE

NEW YORK POST

WEDNESDAY, SEPTEMBER 11, 1996

AT&T SOLUTIONS WINS $1.1B TEXTRON CONTRACT

𝕿𝖍𝖊 𝕾𝖙𝖆𝖗-𝕷𝖊𝖉𝖌𝖊𝖗

WEDNESDAY, DECEMBER 31, 1997

AT&T UNIT FINDS THE RIGHT SOLUTIONS
Networking Division Can Be Nimble as a Start-up—And Therein Lies Its Success

INVESTOR'S BUSINESS DAILY
TUESDAY, MARCH 31, 1998

AT&T OUTSOURCING UNIT
REAPS REWARDS IN SHORT ORDER

FOR RELEASE TUESDAY, AUGUST 30, 1999
AT&T SOLUTIONS' NETWORKING MILESTONES
INCLUDE $2 BILLION OF NEW BUSINESS IN 1999

There's a funny thing about dreams: if you believe in them heart and soul, dare to pursue them full-tilt, and do everything you can to make them come true—the end result is success.

It happened for the start-up AT&T Solutions team, which went from brainstorm to billions-a-year in less than half a decade. The story conjures Walt Disney's starting up with an investment of $500 borrowed from his uncle in 1923. Sure, AT&T Solutions had more than $500 to start with, but considering the risks they took, their jump into IT outsourcing was still a bold leap of faith.

How bold are you?

Are you a dreamer, or are you content with the status quo?

Imagine opening the newspaper next year and beholding this headline:

RECORD REVENUES FOR
[Your company's name here]

Business history is waiting to be written.

Let the dreams begin.

Dream

Chapter

I

What's "New" in the New Economy?

July 1994.

Rick Roscitt was 35,000 feet high in the bright blue sky, eastbound from Los Angeles to New York. Lunch was being served in the first-class cabin, but Rick declined his meal. He even refused a glass of complimentary champagne—he was too busy jotting notes on a legal pad. While leaning over him to serve the next passenger, the flight attendant noticed the words that Rick had written at the top of his first page:

THE NEW GLOBAL ECONOMY

The man next to Rick took his own meal. "What are you writing," he said to Rick, "the great American novel?"

Rick replied, "Something like that."

If this had been a novel, it would have been a gripping one—about global business in transition, propelled by fast-advancing computer and telecommunications technology to the verge of a tightly interconnected,

9

mutually enriching brave new world. Rick's jotted notes alone had that page-turning, best-seller whiff:

> **Limitless access to information.**
>
> **Expanding global markets.**
>
> **Business conducted faster than ever, 24 hours a day, 7 days a week, 365 days a year.**
>
> **The demand to increase top-line revenue growth is speeding the move toward globalization by multinational corporations.**
>
> **The Internet is letting customers worldwide view the same information at the same time—so now they can compare products and prices and complete real-time transactions with the click of a mouse.**
>
> **Privatization coupled with deregulation is increasing market competition.**
>
> **Improvements in voice and data communications technology are both heightening customer service expectations and creating new opportunities for self-service.** [1]

Rick filled page after page, writing furiously, stopping only to flex his hand when it cramped.

Rick had reason to feel pressed. At this moment AT&T was 15 months into its information technology (IT) network management arrangement with Chase Manhattan, still steep on the outsourcing learning curve, still figuring out on the run how to operate in the client's physical location, and still doing only the work that the client had formerly done.

The deal's legal aspects alone were overwhelming enough—especially to AT&T, which had never written or managed one of these long-term, arcane outsourcing contracts before. With so much money changing hands in such a high-risk, high-stakes game, Rick had felt compelled to hire an outside firm that specialized in outsourcing law to be his counsel on the deal.

However brash and bold Rick's wildcat venture might have been, though, he wasn't worried about drilling a dry hole. His continuing talks with prospective network outsourcing customers and with potential industry partners affirmed that a significant—if not enormous—market for IT network outsourcing was being born.

How exactly did these potential clients and partners perceive outsourcing? They saw it as The Yankee Group would later describe it in *Forbes*:

WHAT IS OUTSOURCING?[2]

The Yankee Group defines outsourcing as any service-related purchasing decision by management that includes: work normally done by salaried employees that is consigned to a vendor-supplied service and staff; any specific subset of business-related services with a finite scope; a negotiated agreement with a credible third-party services vendor bound by contractual service-level agreements (SLAs); and a finite contract period of one to three years at the low end and seven to ten years at the high end.

Typical outsourcing arrangements are characterized by many of the following:

- Company transfers staff to vendor.
- Company transfers assets to vendor.
- Deal has cost-containment elements.
- Company gains access to value-added business functionality.
- Company gains access to added levels of skilled expert staff.

Outsourcing's Rise to Fame

Traditionally, well-managed companies are those that keep the ratio between increased revenue and increased operating cost at a favorable level. If revenues decrease, companies usually reduce operating costs as quickly as possible. In the late 1980s and early 1990s, this led to significant downsizing initiatives. But after several rounds of downsizing, companies were approaching critical mass in their staffing requirements. Further reductions threatened their ability to produce products and deliver service.

Outsourcing first appeared in the late 1980s as an alternative—and radically different—way for management to achieve its goals. Early deals emphasized low costs and improved business focus. Companies considered outsourcing only if it could produce the same or better levels of service for savings of 15 percent or greater, thereby reducing the company's operating costs and increasing shareholder value. At the same time, outsourcing freed companies from overseeing the day-to-day operations of certain functions—releasing management to focus on its core business.

As outsourcing proved itself at reducing costs, its usage—and its success rate—soared. The prediction that it would die out as economic conditions improved later in the 1990s was false. Unsuccessful outsourcing arrangements, the by-products of poorly crafted deals or radically altered business models, were the exception rather than the rule.

The Outsourcing Advantage

As their experience grew, corporate managers discovered that there were many more benefits to outsourcing than just low costs and improved business focus. Indeed, the list of advantages expanded to encompass:

- Faster access to global markets through already-in-place support infrastructures, partnerships, or alliances
- Lower costs through larger-volume purchase agreements
- Lower costs by leveraging multicustomer, shared resources (e.g., staff, systems, and facilities)
- Large pools of available, skilled staff that could be deployed as needed to meet immediate business needs
- Improved employee motivation through enhanced career-path alternatives, increased advancement opportunities, increased profit-sharing opportunities, and better training
- Profit center–oriented management
- Better and proven proprietary project management processes and methodologies
- Improved, proprietary systems and support capabilities
- The ability to leverage companywide knowledge and experience through facilities such as "best practices" databases

With the appearance in the late 1980s of the client/server-to-PC/network for processing and distributing information, IT outsourcing specifically arrived. Enhanced computing and distribution capabilities spurred the development of increasingly complex software applications, which created new systems integration of their own. As spending on technology burgeoned, systems integration specialists such as Andersen Consulting, Computer Sciences Corp., IBM Global Services, and Electronic Data Systems reaped huge revenues and high industry repute. Every major corporation in America now needed state-of-the-art information technology to compete in their industries—and expertise in managing it to win.

The Yankee Group also said:

Whether entering new markets, introducing new product lines, or expanding globally, corporate management is under constant pressure to do it better, faster, and cheaper. For those smart enough to make outsourcing a central part of their business strategy, selecting the best providers and crafting favorable deals are critical to staying competitive in the new millennium.

In the early 1990s, skeptics were quick to dismiss the widespread adoption of outsourcing as a passing fad, a management tool du jour whose role would diminish significantly as economic conditions improved. They couldn't have been more wrong.

In fact, outsourcing played an integral role in the rebound of U.S. businesses, freeing management to concentrate on core competencies and become more focused and competitive.

Opportunity Abounds

The economy is booming. The stock market is hitting record highs, unemployment is at record lows—and inflation remains in check. Business is thriving, not only because traditional lines of business are prospering, but also because traditional companies are rapidly reengineering themselves to be different.

Opportunity abounds—but only for those companies flexible enough to react swiftly to changes in market demand. Over the next three years, companies everywhere will be challenged to manage change far beyond the limits of what they've dealt with over the last three decades. Business change will continue to be driven by the "usual suspects"—mergers and acquisitions, deregulation, changing tax laws, governmental regulations, new product and service offerings, and new ways of reaching customers and suppliers (e.g., Internet and extranets). More and more, however, change would be driven by heated global competition. . . . Not surprisingly, companies that can change faster and more efficiently than their competitors will have the best shot at future success.

An Effective Alternative for Managing Change

Outsourcing both business and IT functions can be an extremely effective alternative for implementing the business changes required to gain competitive advantage. At the same time, outsourcing can help companies better utilize internal resources and maximize their control over the change management process.

For example, outsourcers with a broad geographic infrastructure and service capability can immediately provide delivery options for customers wanting to quickly penetrate new global markets. Outsourcers can readily deploy trained experts and experienced staff, thereby eliminating delays in retraining in-house staff or recruiting from the outside. Outsourcers are up to date on the latest methodologies to more efficiently deliver required services. . . .

Looking Ahead

In the years ahead, companies will face significant challenges that threaten their long-term viability: Ever-increasing competition, demand for skilled people, the continuing need for global expansion, the changing regulatory environment, and rigorous bottom-line performance requirements will continue to force managers to quickly reengineer business and IT processes.

The only workable business delivery model that offers the required flexibility and responsiveness to succeed in this environment does seem to be outsourcing. Again and again, outsourcing has proved to be an indispensable management tool—one that will continue to evolve with the times.[3]

In his enthusiasm for outsourcing networking services, Rick wasn't alone. His exhaustive research—and infectious zeal—had persuaded AT&T's president, Alex Mandl, that the company should pursue this market full throttle. Over dinner, Mandl had asked Rick to establish and head a new business unit to do just that.

Rick's answer was, "No."

No? Wasn't this what Rick had been dreaming about doing all along?

Yes, it was, but gearing up and launching a start-up would take all-out, undistracted effort, and Rick had another full-time job at AT&T—generating $8 billion of revenue for their Outbound Business Services.

"I'm sorry," Rick said, "I don't have time to do this the way it has to be done. Who's your second choice for this job?"

"I don't have a second choice."

"Okay, I'll do it," Rick replied.

"We began as 12 people in a conference room," recalls Rick of the original team he assembled to create the new business unit. "Today we're 10,000 people in 60 countries, but back then you could have fit us all in a broom closet. And it felt like a broom closet sometimes. They'd shut us in there and forget about us and lose the key. My biggest fear was that we'd never get out."

It was Chase Manhattan—and specifically Chase's Chief Information Officer (CIO) Doug Williams—who opened the door and, by virtually demanding that Rick and company take over their networking as an outsourcer, beckoned the team to come out.

DOUG WILLIAMS'S STORY: PRESENT AT THE CREATION

I'd gotten very frustrated with my telecom function people. They boasted about saving the company money, but in fact, the function was getting more expensive and the users less happy.

I used to work for ADP. I kidded people at Chase by saying I worked for a for-profit organization before I came to this bank.

The problem was that Chase had the wrong attitude on telecommunications. We were engineering everything because we thought we had to. We were Chase! But at the same time, AT&T was engineering our network, too, to put it into their network. Our huge engineering department and theirs were doing the same thing. That was inefficient and slow. There was no way I could attract top talent to Chase with this going on.

Like any data processing executive with in-house technology silos, I was under pressure to reduce budgets that were growing without anyone knowing why. The trap was to lease more new equipment on three-, four-, or five-year terms and then not be able to change it fast enough to keep up with innovations that were happening day to day.

This was early 1990s: the desktop was just coming out, and every technology person in the company was a self-appointed CIO. Just because they got invited to all the conferences and special vendors' events, they felt important. So they all thought their ways of handling our network were the best.

The only "best" way, I realized, was to hand over the management of our network to AT&T, both the technology plank and the service plank. They just seemed the most capable of handling both. My chairman was hesitant to do anything outside in those days, but I sold him on outsourcing in the end. When AT&T didn't take the job right away, I told them if you don't say yes, I'll get somebody else. They said yes.

The trouble is, they didn't understand how to negotiate a service-type contract that protected both sides and put each in a position of win-win. But Rick hired our outsourcing specialist legal firm to help with these very complex and sticky issues. And he took a firm personal hand himself in pushing the deal through.

None of this would have happened with traditional AT&T. The contract would have gone through layers and layers of committees and legal reviews and the decision would never have gotten made. Rick's approach was let's get the facts on the table, and let's look at them, but let's not analyze them to death. Let's keep pushing, let's not get side-tracked, and let's get this done. And so we did.

More than vendor and client, we were partners after that. AT&T didn't dictate every step. We each deferred to the other when it was appropriate. If partners don't do that, it's not a real partnership, and ours was.

"AT&T Solutions was an idea whose time had come," says Rick, "and the idea came from one of our clients. I always recommend listening to clients. They'll inspire you every time."

"It was a learning experience for both sides," Williams admits.

For AT&T Solutions, the learning curve was a slippery slope, made slicker by difficulties in finding the right people within AT&T to handle the job.

"They struggled a long time on that," says Williams, "especially to find an on-site manager. Then they picked a wonderful guy who turned out to be a terrific representative of AT&T and a great member of Chase. We were lucky they found Gerry Pape."

GERRY PAPE'S STORY, PART 1: CHASE MANHATTAN BANK

I was living in Atlanta at the time, and when they said the new position was in Brooklyn, I had to swallow hard. For 15 years, though, I'd worked for AT&T, which was pretty internally focused. Since I really like working directly with clients in a service environment, I accepted the new job.

I was the first general manager on the first outsourcing engagement we ever had.

One day soon after the contract was signed, I was at the Chase technology center, and I was going to meet with Rick to review the contract and designate personnel to be transferred to the bank. I needed to find paper and a pencil, but I couldn't. We had nothing installed there yet, no PC laptops, no office supplies. Finally, I found some pencils and pads of paper with the Chase logo on them, so I took those and sat in an empty conference room and wrote up the pertinent issues and how we could address them. So you see we were making this up on the fly, there was no preexisting game plan, no training manual, no rules. In the beginning was just the word, you could say, written on the client's stationery with their pencils in our hands. And that was symbolic, I think, of how we were starting from scratch.

At the very start, transport revenue was split $18 million for us, $18 million for MCI. Doug Williams said to me, "If you can give us equal or better service at an equal or better cost, you can take it all." In less than a year we did, and converted all that MCI traffic into AT&T revenue.

I came to work every day as a Chase employee. I was an AT&T employee, too, of course, but I didn't work on AT&T business. I just used AT&T capabilities and staff and support to help Chase.

I worked very hard to be accepted not only by Doug Williams but also by his direct reports. I would go to his staff meetings, and my office was right down the hall. That built credibility and trust.

I think the general manager job is a combination of coordinating the relationship, facilitating the technology, and—since we own the P&L (profit and loss)—overseeing the finance. We lead clients to where they want to go under the contract's requirements, and then take them even further as well.

A big lesson from Chase was how desperately networks need bandwidth on demand. Not in 30-day, 60-day, 90-day intervals, but instantly. Architectures must be created to build that capacity because customers today want everything without delay.

It's like New York City itself: demanding, in your face, abrupt. If you're not ready for it, you can feel abused. If you can't meet the challenges, you can get run down. To me, it was like a foreign country at first, so different from where I grew up in southern Illinois.

But I got to like it. Now I find the intensity and the pace of the city refreshing. I appreciate the honest, no-nonsense talk because it lets you know where you stand. People hold nothing back, whereas in the Midwest folks are more reluctant to be confrontational. Traditional AT&T culture is like that: you're more encouraged to restrain your feelings in order to get along. It's appropriate that Chase's tech center is in Brooklyn. The environment suits their style.

I said earlier that pencil and paper were good symbols of how we started. Here's some more symbolism: the Chase deal began on April Fools' Day, 1994, and AT&T Solutions was officially launched on Valentine's Day, 1995, which means we went from fooling around to love in a year. That's not bad.

Finally, I'll say this: as much as anyone, Doug Williams launched AT&T Solutions. He wanted to do outsourcing and he gave us a call. In his mind, it was the right concept at the right time, and we were the right company to make it happen. And he was right.

While the Chase project proceeded, the AT&T Solutions team went to meet with such potential consulting partners as Andersen Consulting, IBM, and CSC.

As Rick tells it, "Our message to them was, 'We're heading into this business in a pretty big way, so let's talk openly and directly about whether we should partner or not. We don't want to steal your piece of the pie. We want to work with you to make the pie bigger.' They listened to us, more politely than seriously it turned out, then said, 'Who needs you?'"

Undeterred, the team assiduously studied these companies' field operations, internal organizations, training programs, and marketing strategies. "When we saw something we really liked, we used it," Rick remembers. "We didn't copy. We borrowed, mimicked, synthesized, and distilled. We realized that to become unique we had to start as an amalgam. To create our own identity, we had to stir up a lot of existing elements, then add ourselves to the mix."

Research proceeded for three more months, until Rick's notes for each interview went from 25 pages to less than one. "I'd heard what I needed to hear," he says. "Now it was time to get to work—to parlay the single job with Chase into a full enterprise."

Back in the "broom closet," the AT&T Solutions team affirmed the working values that would form every step AT&T Solutions took.

"We rallied around what clients would need," says Mary Ellen Caro, one of the original 12 team members and now vice president and chief operating officer (COO) of AT&T Data Internet Services. "And we specified what made us, as outsourcers, unique. Our working values today are the same as then: 24/7 customer focus, a commitment to continual professional development, and openness to diversity of thought. We vowed to run AT&T Solutions as a distinctly spirited enterprise, and to manage every engagement as a business of its own. While setting ourselves massive challenges, we promised to support and protect each other and make sure we didn't burn out."

Values would keep the ship on course, but how would the ship itself actually look?

On a flip chart, Rick wrote the burning questions of the day:

WHO IS IT WE
WANT TO BE?

DO WE WANT TO LOOK LIKE ONE OF THE OTHER BIG
PLAYERS?
(OR ALL OF THEM TOGETHER?)

IS THIS A LOT OF WORK FOR "SO WHAT"?
(WILL AT&T CARE?
WILL SHAREHOLDERS??
WILL THE MARKETPLACE???)[4]

"Everyone had answers to the questions," says Rick, "and plenty of research data to back up their points of view. But no proof. We were all dreaming there in that room, and believing, and daring ourselves to give it a shot. But to prove we were onto something worthwhile, we had to get out of that room and go out there and do it."

Which meant another leap of faith.

Fortunately, faith was something the group of 12 had plenty of—even though many people at AT&T did not. Faith, though, is not negotiable paper. "We needed gold to back it up," says Rick. "Something we could hold and wave in the air. A charter, an affirmation, a call to arms." A mission statement, in short.

"We realized," continues Rick, "that to take this leap of faith we had to justify the faith—first to ourselves so we could then justify it to the world."

In the beginning, indeed, is the word: "and the first words," Rick asserts, "had to be about the business and economic environment of the day—the state of information technology, the challenges, the opportunities, the problems, and the solutions (*solutions*—nice word). And that's why I was there writing about 'The New Global Economy' on that flight from LA to New York."

"There's some turbulence up ahead," the captain now said over the cabin speakers as Rick flipped over a new page, "so I'll be turning on the Fasten Seat Belt sign. Meanwhile, we'll be climbing to a higher altitude to find calmer air."

Rick didn't even hear the announcement; he was "in the zone," pouring his heart and mind out in ink:

> **Traditionally, an economy has been the management of resources in an essentially stand-alone local, national, or continental context. The primary indicators of an economy's health have been keyed to the production, distribution, and consumption of commodities—essentially hard goods. In the new economy, resources will transcend goods and services to include information, which is transformed into knowledge-based relationships.**
>
> **To compete[5]**

Rick crossed out "compete" and wrote, "thrive," then crossed out "thrive" and wrote:

> **To SURVIVE, companies must:**
>
> - **Strengthen electronic bonds to customers with real-time access to information, products, and services.**
> - **Be able to conduct electronic commerce anywhere in the world, at any time, day or night.**
> - **Use the new technology to become more responsive to markets, achieve higher productivity, and outperform the competition.**
>
> **Infrastructure will become increasingly dominated by desktop services.**

It will be increasingly difficult to retain world-class network management expertise.

The trend toward a peripatetic workforce will necessitate new and better ways of communicating.

With the burgeoning of the Internet, radio frequency, and cellular—and with servers becoming cheaper and more stable—how can companies evaluate and implement the new developments fast enough? How can they keep up? How can they focus on their core businesses and manage the infrastructure that supports them at the same time?

Answer: They CAN'T—on their own.

How can they do all their own planning and systems management on a global, holistic basis?

Answer: They CAN'T—without expert help.[6]

Rick lifted his pen, then set it down again to note one more thought:

"Economy has frequently nothing to do with the money being spent, but with the wisdom used in spending it." Henry Ford[7]

Rick looked up from his writing and noticed the passenger seated next to him was reading over Rick's shoulder.

"So what's your novel about?" asked the passenger.

"It's not a novel, actually. It's notes for a new business."

"A new business? In what field, if I may ask?"

"Information technology, telecommunications."

"What's the name of your new business?"

"We don't know yet."

"What will you be making?"

"We'll be service providers, offering IT systems management and consulting on an outsourcing basis."

The man said, "Hmm" and fell silent. Rick figured that was the end of this conversation. He resumed writing, but his pen had run dry. As he searched for another, the passenger said, "Here, use mine."

"Thanks. I'm Rick Roscitt, by the way. I'm with AT&T." The passenger introduced himself and Rick got back to work.

Finally, the plane leveled off. "IT systems consulting, eh?" said the passenger as the jolting stopped. "That's a growing phenomenon, I've heard."

"It's about 35 percent of a $50 billion worldwide outsourcing market today. I'd predict that in three years, it'll be more than 40 percent of an $80 billion market."

"Who else is in it right now?"

"Andersen Consulting is a big, full-service information technology shop, and IBM Global Services runs data centers and servers. But we're aiming to focus on networking. Of course it'll be hard to get the first set of clients to believe in us, but the AT&T brand name will help."

"Sounds like a great business story in the making."

"Five, six years from now it'd make a great book."

"What would you call the book?" asked the passenger.

"Why? Do you want to write it?"

"It looks like you've already started it," said the man, nodding at Rick's notes. "What's the first chapter about?"

"The state of business communications in the new global economy."

"Tell me more about that."

And so, as they crossed the American heartland, Rick summarized what he'd written so far, explaining that it was the preamble to a mission statement he was writing—his "manifesto," as he called it—for his 12-member start-up team. The passenger nodded periodically but said little. Somewhere over Missouri he interjected: "One question."

"Shoot."

"What will it take for companies to win in this new economy?"

Rick smiled, flipped to a blank page on his pad, and said, "I was just coming to that."

DEBRIEFING

Vision

Chase Manhattan Bank couldn't see through the tangle of its own network. The AT&T Solutions team saw, if not the immediate technological solution, then the possibility that a solution could be devised. They looked telescopically out over the sea of shining potential. Then, with their bearings fixed, they trained their microscopic lenses on the problem at hand—and got to work.

"AT&T Solutions was an idea whose time had come," said Rick.

Many good ideas come and go, however, before they are seen as timely and profitable. They are not *seen* as opportunities, so they become opportunities missed. Why? Because people's vision is often not acute, or is focused the wrong way.

The vision of this start-up team was laser-sharp.

It was also wide-ranging and probing, as the team's exhaustive research, self-questioning, and self-refining attest.

The AT&T Solutions vision was also as nimble as it was cutting edge—a good thing since in this era the view changes as fast as the eye can blink.

What does the vision of AT&T Solutions teach you?

That business vision isn't just an optical function—it's what you eat, sleep, walk, talk, live, and breathe as well. It's what's out there—and what's in you, too. It's an IMAX journey to the far galaxies of entrepreneurial possibility, and a journey to the center of your company's soul.

From the receptionist to the CEO, everyone must make the trip—naysayers and ankle biters, too. These doubters will come along in time, once they can see as well as you do.

Your job is to clear their view and then direct their efforts toward making your dream come true. In the process, make sure to bring your suppliers and customers into line with your point of view. They're key members of your overall business team, too.

Here, in broad terms, is how to start:

Reinvent Your Product or Service

- Don't just make your product or deliver your service, remake your customers' experience of buying it. (List 10 ways this can be done.)
- Make customers feel well informed and confident in their decisions, not pressured, manipulated, or duped.
- Realize that in reinventing your customers' experience, you are reinventing yourself.

Communicate Your Vision

You're in the wheelhouse of your company's ship, spyglass trained on the horizon.

A spout appears. "Thar she blows!" you cry out.

Now you have to make sure that no one stays below. Whaling is massive work, and demands a full crew. In business terms, this means presenting the vision to all stakeholders—employees, stockholders, suppliers, and customers, too.

"Prepare to head up! Trim sails! All hands to whaling stations!"

Once you've set your course and communicated your vision, you must do it again and again. It's hard to hear clearly on the high seas of the new economy while you're being blasted by the screaming wind. Out here, messages have to be repeated eight times before they sink in.

Be persistent and consistent. Never waver, never compromise, don't quibble point-by-point. Once the vision is set, it's not negotiable. It's no longer time to debate.

Get All Hands on Deck

Not everyone will buy in all at once, but they'll all have to in the end. Because without a razor-sharp, universally embraced vision, you're not just sailing blindly, you're sailing without a rudder. You're dead.

Checklist of Further Actions

___ Write a press story that announces and details your own dream coming true.

___ Itemize your available resources in terms of money and personnel.

___ Do a gut-check to determine if you and your team have the courage, strength, and competence to start the journey and stay the course.

___ Affirm that you are ready, willing, and able not just to dream but to believe, dare, and do to make your dream come true.

___ Assess the value your dream will likely bring to your organization.

___ If pursuing your vision will be a leap of faith, justify your faith to yourselves with exhaustive research, a mission statement, and an affirmation of collective will.

___ Beat the bushes within your organization to marshal support for your vision.

___ Honestly decide whether you are a dreamer or are snug with the status quo.

___ Itemize the opportunities that the new fast-paced global economy presents for you.

___ Assess your ability to reengineer your business and its processes to meet the following challenges:

    ___ Intensifying domestic and global competition

    ___ Growing demand for skilled employees

    ___ The changing regulatory environment

    ___ Rigorous bottom-line performance requirements

___ If you are under pressure to reduce rising budgets, make sure you know why you are.

___ Escape from an in-house technology silo mentality so you can see the potential of outsourcing in a big-picture view.

___ Determine your ability to change your equipment fast enough to keep up with innovation's fast pace.

___ Examine your decision-making process: Does it involve layers of committees and legal reviews? If so, streamline the process so facts are laid out, reviewed, and acted upon—without being analyzed to death.

___ Study, synthesize, and distill your competitors' strategies and operations so you can match their strengths in the marketplace and develop unique features to set you apart.

___ Listen to your customers' criticisms as well as their praise for your performance, and note their constructive suggestions and advice.

___ Stay attuned to your customers' needs and requirements, and make customer satisfaction your 24/7 rallying cry.

___ Commit to continual professional development.

___ Affirm an unequivocal openness to diversity of thought.

___ While setting yourselves massive challenges, protect yourselves from overextending beyond human capacity and burning out.

___ Ask yourselves these questions:

    ___ Who is it we want to be?

    ___ Do we want to look like one of the other players? (Or all of them together?)

___ Is this a lot of work for "so what"? (Will your company care? Will your shareholders? Will the marketplace?)

___ Remember: "Economy has frequently nothing to do with the money spent, but with the wisdom used in spending it." Set your sights on soaring profits, but keep your head on tight.

2

What Does It Take to Win in the New Economy?

"Networking." As Rick spoke the word, he wrote it in capitals on his pad. "To succeed in the next millennium, businesses will have to adopt networking as a central component of their corporate strategies. Or I should say, 'value-driven networking'—networking that integrates the business model with social and technological changes that are facing the global marketplace. Networking with a definite purpose."

"To grow profits," said Rick's fellow passenger.

"To grow them in a new, enlightened way—not just by using hardware and software to link users and computer resources, but by pursuing the whole spectrum of activities, disciplines, skills, and objectives that are needed to maintain competitive advantage in a communications-intensive world."

"Because to stand in place is to fall behind, right?" the passenger asked.

"Exactly. We can't look at networks just as physical infrastructures anymore. We can't just hook up distant users, databases, and applications and leave it at that. That's the old way. That's treating networks as static, well-behaved systems that link low-maintenance users to stable computing environments. That's networking as a noun."

"A noun?"

"As opposed to a verb. But a noun shouldn't oppose a verb, it should be the subject of the verb."

"Pardon me?"

"A sentence has a subject and predicate—a noun and its action. Right? The new definition of networking does, too. To fully achieve and profit from networking, a company must master networking both as a noun and a verb."

"And the noun in this case is . . . ?"

"All of the physical 'stuff' connected to the transport facility: the hardware, software, glue-ware, routers, servers, hubs, and the full variety of end-user devices. The tangible things you can see and touch. It's what everyone associates with the physical network—telecommunications, wide area networks, or WANs, local area networks, or LANs, the Internet, and the new extranets and intranets."

"So what is networking as a verb?"

"Networking the verb is logical as well as physical. It's what one does with the noun, how the physical networking can be designed to create and sustain a hierarchy of business value that includes networking integration, mobility, work-group collaboration, knowledge management, optimized resource management for financial performance, and e-commerce."

"And if you leave out the verb—"

"Then there's no action. There's promise but no delivery and hence, no results. You have all these sophisticated networks without specific business objectives. You have investment without strategy. You have wishful thinking instead of a value-driven business plan, and a plan that's not driven by value can't produce value."[1]

The passenger began to speak, but Rick spoke first: "You want to know how networking produces value? How it increases corporate worth at all levels?"

The passenger smiled. "As a matter of fact, I do."

Rick lifted his pen and drew a pyramid on the pad.

"Look at this," Rick said. "The challenge of growing market value is like climbing steep slopes toward a pinnacle. New-economy networking will drive inherent value all along the way—at the bottom by promoting network efficiency that lowers internal costs, and further up by facilitating communication and transactions between companies and their customers, opening up new markets, boosting top-line revenue growth, and sustaining competitive advantage. Not all companies will finish the ascent. Some will feel satisfied to stop partway, but the potential for value creation will be limitless for those who push all the way to the top."

Rick showed his rough sketch to the passenger (see Exhibit 1).

"Disneyland," said the passenger, regarding Rick's pyramid-shaped drawing.

"Excuse me?" said Rick.

"Your drawing there, what you're talking about, reminds me of the Matterhorn at Disneyland. I was just there this week. It has steep slopes, a sharp pinnacle, and all that."

Rick looked at his simple sketched triangle shape. "Sure, okay."

"Not just the Matterhorn but the whole Disney story—the inspiration, the vision, the work ethic, the drive for success. Walt Disney once said," the passenger continued, "'I dream, I test my dreams against my beliefs, I dare to take risks, and I execute my vision to make those dreams come true.' It sounds like you're doing just that."

"We're dreaming and believing, anyway," replied Rick. "And we've dared to sign up Chase Manhattan as a first customer, but there's an awful lot we still have to do."

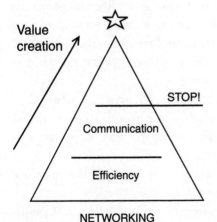

Exhibit 1 A re-creation of Rick's New-Economy Networking Pyramid

"When you look ahead five years, what do you see?" asked the passenger.

Rick set aside his notepad for the first time during the flight. "Networks will become precious vessels," he said, as if telling a sci-fi tale, "that will connect corporate users, suppliers, and current and potential customers around the world. Multibillion dollar transactions will take place over the Internet between any two points on the globe in less time than it takes to [Rick snapped his fingers] do that."

"So in essence," said the passenger, "networking will become the business."

"Yes, and networking will unleash the value of assets and relationships within and beyond the enterprise. A healthy networking-centric environment will become the prevailing measure of a company's value and the measure of its ability to effectively engage in the new world of Electronic Business Communities (EBCs) wherein each firm will be networking for strategic advantage. The EBCs' value-chain connection will speed communications and business transactions, and these can be engaged or discontinued at will."

"What industries are operating in EBCs right now?"

"PC product manufacturing, auto retailing, electronic publishing, electronic banking, and brokerage. It's a growing list. Opportunities for new wealth are being created almost overnight as supply chain costs are slashed and products' time-to-market is decreased. On-demand customer service is becoming the norm. Business partners are accessing intellectual assets how and when they choose. Online companies are finding new ways of using network components, while established businesses are liberating assets that were heretofore undervalued or hard to access. The old rules of competition are going right out the window. With networking it's a whole new game."[2]

"What happens to physical storefronts?" the passenger asked.

"They won't be needed. Businesses won't have to locate in demographically correct geographic sites; they'll invest in networking instead."

"So market leaders will be determined by how well they plan and execute networking-centric strategies," said the passenger.

"And these strategies will free trapped value," agreed Rick. "Companies will thrive by constantly reinventing themselves through advanced networking to meet customers' and business partners' changing needs.

These companies won't see networking as a cost of doing business, but as a strategic enabler of competitive success." (See Exhibit 2.)

"The paradox of the new economy," Rick went on, "will be that the more power you give away, the more powerful you will become."

The passenger, intrigued by the idea of a paradox, asked, "How is that?"

"If you're networking, you can't be dictating. Networking isn't just broadcasting, like on TV or radio, and it's not like the mail—it's a listening medium, too, and when you're listening, you're granting equal value to other people's points of view."

"It's a two-way street."

"More than just two-way. You're interacting with your employees, suppliers, customers, and any other interested parties. You're transacting business, but just as importantly, you're gaining feedback on price, quality, competitiveness, service satisfaction, new product ideas, and new segment notions. That's solid-gold information coming through the wires. Networking tunes you in."

Rick signaled the flight attendant and finally took his lunch. "Amazing how much extra you pay for good food and stainless steel utensils in first class. Free drinks? Considering the ticket price, an in-flight drink costs fifty bucks!"

Spreading some caviar on a cracker, Rick noted that preferred customer service has traditionally meant lavish treatment. Companies seek

The Network: From the Computer Room to the Board Room

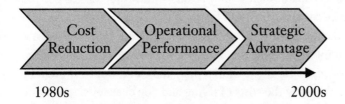

- **New and Emerging Applications Are Networking Centric**
- **Networks Are Becoming Increasingly Complex**
- **Boundary Between Networks & Applications Is Blurring**

Exhibit 2 The Network: From the Computer Room to the Board Room

to distinguish themselves by offering personalized attention, customized plans, convenient geographic locations, and attractive, comfortable places of business to make their customers feel like pampered guests.

"That's what Disney does, too," said the passenger. "The Disney organization treats its customers as guests. In fact, I think they were one of the very first to refer to each and every visitor as a guest."

"Ah, back to the Matterhorn!"

"It's great. It helps the guests enjoy the show, and makes them feel special. It works."

"Sure," said Rick, "but today people are increasingly happy to help themselves on their own time and in their own way. It may be over the phone to an automated technical help desk, or through an order tracking system, or a transactional process system. My point is that traditional customer service, treating customers like guests if you will, won't be the same in the self-service networking age."

"But won't self-service options make customers feel even more like guests—guests with new freedoms of choice in the kind of service they can get?"

"Of course. You're right. That's one of the social implications of networking, and this has to synchronize with the technology drivers and the business strategies, as this self-service, on-demand, real-time economy comes to life. All this has to happen fluidly, and networking will make it flow. Change in one area requires adjustment in all others. If you're stuck in the mud, or if you're rigid, you're dead. Or at least you're way out in the cold. What we're looking for is both high-tech and high-touch." (See Exhibit 3.)

"How will companies know they're out in the cold?" asked the passenger. "Maybe some of them will be too insulated to notice for awhile."

"Some companies are already feeling the chill. The ones who've installed multiple computer systems at a breakneck pace over recent years, but now can't tie them all together, and can't even run each one efficiently, can't justify the costs of trying and don't see much possibility of ultimate success. They're overwhelmed. Despite all their investment in IT and huge staffs, they can't keep up with rapid-fire technological changes. They can't meet rising customer demands for faster and better service. What they want to do, or what they need to do, is focus on their core businesses. They need to bring their products to market and forget about managing the supporting infrastructure. So what's the solution?"

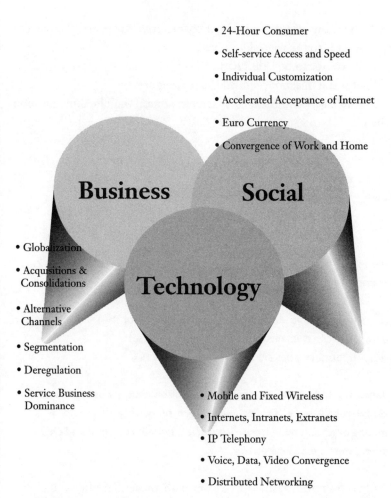

- 24-Hour Consumer
- Self-service Access and Speed
- Individual Customization
- Accelerated Acceptance of Internet
- Euro Currency
- Convergence of Work and Home

Business

Social

- Globalization
- Acquisitions & Consolidations

Technology

- Alternative Channels
- Segmentation
- Deregulation
- Service Business Dominance
- Mobile and Fixed Wireless
- Internets, Intranets, Extranets
- IP Telephony
- Voice, Data, Video Convergence
- Distributed Networking

Exhibit 3 The New, Real-Time Economy Drivers

"You."

"Right. An outsourcing specialist to manage their communications networking. To take over the planning, installation, and operation of these systems on a global, holistic scale."

"Welcome to New York," said the flight attendant over the cabin speakers.

New York? The passenger, so caught up in Rick's story, hadn't even been aware that the plane had started its descent.

"Here's my card," said Rick. "And if you ever want to write that book, let me know."

"With all this drama and cast of characters," suggested the passenger, "it sounds to me more like a play."

"To be or not to be," said Rick.

"That is the question," added the passenger.

"Oh, we'll *be*," said Rick, "that's not the question. The only question is when."

DEBRIEFING

Values

The Random House College Dictionary defines "value" as follows:

value, n., 1. attributed or relative worth, merit, or usefulness. 2. monetary worth.

This quantitative definition guided AT&T Solutions' vision quest to grow profits for its customers as well as for itself.

The dictionary goes on to say the following:

value, n., 3. an ideal, custom, or institution that arouses an emotional response. 4. Ethics. any object or quality desirable as a means or as an end in itself. 5. a spiritual quality of mind and character; moral excellence.

AT&T Solutions framed its vision with those definitions, too. By using ideals, spiritual qualities, and moral excellence to steer their enterprise, they set a true course toward achieving success. And when they ultimately achieved it, as we shall see—they did have an emotional response.

Roy Disney, Walt Disney's brother, said, "When values are clear, decisions are easy."

This means that once values are understood, they sell themselves. To whom do they sell themselves? First—in the ideal, spiritual, moral, and financial sense—to the members of your organization. Second—in terms of monetary worth—to your customer base. In this way, all definitions of value are fulfilled, and everyone is satisfied financially—and emotionally!

Try the following dramatic exercise to help establish values in your organization. Supply your leadership team with paper, pens/pencils, a flip chart, and markers. Explain that you are gathered to establish values that will guide the company to success in the new economy. Then use the following step-by-step procedure:

- Ask each member of the team to list his or her three to five most important values.
- Ask the team members to pair up.
- Have the members of each pair present and discuss their respective lists. Then have them jointly create a single new list of three to five values.
- Assemble all the team members into groups of four.
- Have the members of the new groups discuss their respective new lists. Then request that each four-member group create a single list.
- Continue assembling team members into twice-as-large groups (of eight, then sixteen, etc.) until the maximum-sized group is reached. Each new group should create its own new list.
- With the whole leadership team, reach consensus on the final list of three to five company values.

Debrief by asking the following:

- Did the process lead to the best set of values?
- Was there unanimous agreement on the final list of values? If not, were the sacrifices and compromises worth the result?
- What did you observe about values listed by individuals, as compared to those established by larger and larger groups?
- In your own company position, could you support and be guided by today's final list of values? Why or why not?

To cascade values throughout the organization,

- Repeat the above exercise at the next level in the organization.
- Compare results with leadership team values.
- Reconcile differences between levels and repeat the procedure with the next level.

Note: This process should proceed efficiently if you have four or fewer organizational levels. If you have more than four levels, don't bother with the exercise, since with that degree of bureaucracy you'll never compete at the speed of change!

Lesson: Values are manna, but they can't be force-fed. They must be cultivated organically in the rich soil of the enterprise, judiciously thinned as they proliferate, and then harvested at their peak.

Chapter 3

AT&T's Winning Start-up Solution

Whether 'tis nobler in the mind to suffer

The slings and arrows of outrageous fortune

Or to take arms against a sea of troubles

And by opposing, end them.

—Hamlet

What troubles would the AT&T Solutions start-up unit face? Would its business fortune be outrageous or kind?

To sleep—perchance to dream . . .

One thing was sure: there was no "perchance" about Rick Roscitt—he was dreaming in wide-screen, high definition, and surround sound.

But while Rick and his team believed in his dream, would the world believe in it when the enterprise was finally born?

And would it be born at all? Would big, conservative Ma Bell treat this start-up as an unwanted child—and abort? Would their zeal be tempered, or totally snuffed out, by corporate rationality? Would mother AT&T, to protect its venerable "stock for widows and orphans," devour its own unborn young?

> ... conscience does make cowards of us all,

said Hamlet.

> And thus the native hue of resolution
>
> Is sicklied o'er with the pale cast of thought,
>
> And enterprises of great pitch and moment
>
> With this regard their currents turn awry
>
> And lose the name of action.

What a shame it would be if Rick's dream play lost its name of action, never made it through the Believe, Dare, and Do stages, and thus closed before its opening night.

The fact that an audience for the play did seem to be emerging, though, gave hope. More and more big firms were doing spin-offs, carve-outs, sell-offs, and privatizations—in short, they were breaking up and restructuring their assets to focus on their core competencies.

These moves were paying off. A J.P. Morgan study called "Corporate Clarity" showed that firms focusing on what they did best outperformed firms that diversified by 20 percent. As e-business burgeoned, one could predict that these companies would compete against each other less as individual entities than as internetworked groups. A consequent need for outsourced IT systems management would be a logical and inevitable result.

An interesting corollary to the breakup trend was a move to competing globally by bulking up—not by packing on more upstream weight but by vertically integrating downstream around one or a few competencies to get closer to the customer. As the upstream processes were "deverticalized," the need to outsource them could be expected to increase. As the firms grew larger and internal transaction costs rose, the marginal, financially draining noncore activities would need to be eliminated for economy's sake.

And who would then undertake these eliminated activities?

Outsourcers, of course.

And how would companies decide which activities should be handed over to these outside experts?

They would identify the two or three things they did better than anyone else in the world, commit to pursuing these single-mindedly, and then outsource everything else.

And which outsourcer should they pick? (A no-brainer here.)

The one that specialized in networking.

The one that could power clients into the new global economy, remake their technology platforms, and revamp their operations to boost their bottom lines, increase their market shares, and lift their businesses to new heights.[1]

The one with the expertise and the proven, state-of-the-art technology to back its promises up.

The one, in short, with the winning solutions.

Six months later, the passenger picked up *The Wall Street Journal* and saw this:

AT&T SETS UP UNIT TO MANAGE COMPUTER NETWORKS FOR CLIENTS
Concern Faces Major Rivals in Push for Larger Stake in "Outsourcing" Business

AT&T Corp., aiming to become a bigger player in the booming market for "outsourcing" of computer services, set up a quasi-autonomous unit to manage corporate clients' worldwide networks. . . .

To jump-start the new business, called AT&T Solutions, AT&T is assigning to it 5,000 employees, a backlog of more than $1 billion in orders, and more than 100 corporate clients. . . .

AT&T confirmed that it has hired a top Unisys executive, Victor Millar, who helped build Andersen Consulting, to head AT&T Solutions as president and chief executive. Reporting to Mr. Millar as the unit's chief operating officer will be AT&T veteran Richard Roscitt, who will be vice president and general manager.

The New York Times added this note:

> **AT&T said Great Western Bank, the second-largest savings unit in the United States, had signed a seven-year, $160 million contract with AT&T Solutions. The company said it expects to announce more contracts shortly.**

"More contracts shortly"—in other words, stay tuned for future developments. However, with 5,000 employees and 100 clients inherited from AT&T, plus the Chase Manhattan and Great Western accounts, the present looked pretty well set.

Or did it?

ComputerWorld reported the following:

> **Susan Scrupski, editor of "Info-Server," an outsourcing newsletter in Barnegat, NJ, said she does not believe AT&T's new unit will have trouble coordinating with other parts of AT&T. More problematic may be its relations with IBM, EDS, and Computer Sciences Corp.—all major customers as well as partners with AT&T on outsourcing contracts. "Absolutely, it'll cause bad blood," Scrupski said.**

Scrupski's prediction came true the next day, when the following story appeared in *The New York Times:*

> **The AT&T Corporation's entry into computer services has provoked one of its largest customers, Electronic Data Systems, to threaten to look elsewhere rather than do business with a competitor. . . . "I must say, AT&T keeps on making it more difficult for us to continue being a large customer of theirs," said Gary J. Fernandez, an EDS senior vice president.**

Apparently, outsourcing had the potential to make strange, if not incompatible, bedfellows. Would AT&T Solutions and its future customers and partners unite for better or for worse and in sickness and in health—or end up divorced? Would their business marriages be made in heaven or hell?

The New York Times went on:

> In response to EDS, Richard Roscitt, the chief operating officer of
> AT&T Solutions, said, "To overreact to our announcement on any-
> one's part is irrational. We're a big customer of EDS as well, and we
> have no intention of wholesale dismissing EDS from our services. . . .
> We're not trying to replicate ourselves to be another EDS."

Indeed, far from trying to replicate anyone else's business model, AT&T Solutions was endeavoring to forge an identity that was unique.

"To wannabe or not to wannabe" was not their cosmic question. "To be or not to be ourselves—and to live or die on our own merits" was.

Of course, they expected to live.

But how would they? How would this newborn enterprise, conceived in dreams, grow strong on the nourishing milk of belief?

The curtain had fallen on AT&T Solutions' Act One—but as F. Scott Fitzgerald said, there are no second acts in America. So how would AT&T Solutions build the reputation, corporate culture, and alliances to prove Fitzgerald's words false?

DEBRIEFING

Vision/Values

AT&T Solutions demonstrated the value of vision, as well as the vision inherent in its values. They showed that vision and values are linked.

The moral for you is this:

With clear vision you may see where you are going, but without strong, well-articulated values, it may not be worth making the trip.

Are you a visionary? Are your dreams bringing value to your organization and to your customers in every sense?

The following counterpointed efforts will ensure that the interests of *all* stakeholders intersect:

Vision	Value
• Dream in wide-screen, high definition, and surround sound.	• Keep your eyes on the road ahead.
• Align your organization with your vision.	• Affirm an unequivocal commitment to diversity of thought.
• Align all members of your organization toward common goals.	• Involve all stakeholders in developing processes, clarify process ownership, refine interfaces between steps, and use language that everyone understands.
• Hire the best and brightest personnel.	• Commit to continual professional development; invest in your people's success.
• Meet massive challenges.	• Protect yourself and your associates from overextending beyond human capacity and burning out.
• Perform at peak levels.	• Achieve peak performance by aligning toward shared goals and affirming a collective will to succeed.
• Achieve mutual trust among members of your organization.	• Earn mutual trust by communicating openly and honestly and by following through on commitments.
• Make effective, timely decisions.	• Clarify issues, refine their scope, involve the right people in the discussion, stay focused on the facts, reaffirm priorities, narrow the list of alternatives, and achieve consensus in choosing the best one.
• Strategize to achieve competitive success.	• Communicate your strategy to all members of your organization, get them to buy in, and then rally them behind your action plan.
• Grow profits at record rates.	• Grow profits by putting your customers' interests first.
• Aim for 100 percent customer satisfaction.	• Engage customers in a dialogue about their needs instead of selling them a bill of goods.
• Lead your enterprise at the speed of change.	• Give your customers customized attention in the self-service, on-demand, real-time, new economy.
• Be the best of the best in your industry.	• Focus on two or three core competencies and outsource the rest.
• Work harder and smarter than your competition; achieve outstanding success.	• Have fun at work; celebrate success.
• Dream of a golden future.	• Believe, Dare, and Do to make your dream come true.

PART II

Believe

4

Building a Winning Reputation

"I don't get no respect," said Rodney Dangerfield.

Rick Roscitt, reflecting on his unit's "orphan" status within AT&T, could say the same thing. But in 1995 Rick wasn't complaining, just noting a temporary situation that he was determined to change by building his client roster.

Gaining respect through clients while still needing clients to gain respect, however, is any start-up's classic catch-22. How is it overcome? How does a new company establish market credibility when its collateral, in lieu of proven success, is merely its word?

"With any firm you start," says Rick, "it's difficult to get the first set of clients to trust in you, but you've got to get the first clients."

What client, though, would contract an IT services firm without consulting other companies for which that firm had worked?

AT&T hadn't worked for any companies as an IT outsourcer when Chase Manhattan sought its services in 1993, yet the bank trusted that the relationship would bear fruit. "I'll always be indebted to them," says Rick. "They certainly took a leap of faith."[1]

What inspired and grounded Chase's faith? What powered their leap?

First, AT&T acknowledged the experimental nature of the project by entering a shared-risk relationship with Chase, as opposed to a fixed-price contract. In the arrangement, costs would be shared as long as they remained stable, but the bank would pay more if costs went up and less if costs went down. Second, AT&T refrained from dictating how the work would be done, and committed to a frank, two-way problem-solving exchange.[2]

They know that a lot of things can be generated in a lab, but visiting and talking to clients is what really makes the creative sparks fly.

"Their senior team sat down with us," says Denis O'Leary, Chase's current executive vice president. "They heard our concerns, and they listened to our point of view. They handled themselves very professionally during that period; they earned big points with us. By staying in close touch, they maintained our trust."

Still, as a networking services outsourcer, AT&T was finding its way, and trust had to be built day by day.

"We were sort of a Beta customer," says O'Leary. "AT&T was refining its outsourcing act. It wasn't yet running like a Swiss watch."

That's an understatement, which O'Leary quickly amends. "Actually, they were more like a blender running at high speed."

A blender?

"Churning up ingredients, mixing them, chopping them."

This is typical of dotcom start-ups, O'Leary notes, even those spinning off from big corporations. "With Rick's unit, there was constant change and ambiguity," he recalls. "It was chaos, mixed with panic and fear. Dotcom start-ups live on the cusp of disaster, guided by their fear. Motivated by it, in fact. Fear that they'll run out of cash. Fear that they'll flop. Fear that their competition will get a killer deal before they do. But the other element is a true 24/7 commitment to work, and for all their employees that means farewell to a balanced life. Forget vacations, forget personal time, and forget weekends off. It's all gone. The business proposition comes first. It's a rare group of people who will commit themselves to that, to life in that blender. Big companies don't. But Rick and his team did."

"We wanted a strategic partnership," says Chase's Doug Williams, somewhat more matter-of-factly.

With AT&T treating Chase as an ally as much as a client, and working 24/7 to turn the blender into a Swiss watch, that's exactly what the bank got. With Chase signed up, AT&T was not a totally unknown entity as an IT outsourcer when Great Western Bank became client number two in 1994—choosing AT&T over EDS. (Great Western was the second contract AT&T Solutions won on its own, as distinct from the back accounts inherited from AT&T.)

For Great Western, AT&T Solutions set up a nationwide, high-speed, end-to-end "frame-relay" communications and computer network linking the bank's more than 560 offices and 550 ATM machines in 23 states. It also agreed to manage all LANs and WANs from the bank's operations center in Northridge, California.

"They did it in a very tight time line," says Jesse King, Great Western's senior vice president, who expected the bank to save about $30 million over the life of the contract.

"We were convinced that AT&T had the best technologies, as well as a demonstrated ability to pull it all together," King goes on. "Our business's vision is highly dependent on technology, and I had complete confidence that AT&T would provide us with state-of-the-art technologies now and in the future. Our past relationship with AT&T, and the creativity they applied to our business, made them a trusted partner."

Notice that, like Chase's Doug Williams, King called AT&T a "partner," not a vendor. "I can imagine no better ally than AT&T to address a telecommunications challenge of our scale," said Donald R. Hollis, executive vice president of The First National Bank of Chicago. Hollis was happy because an AT&T-managed network helped First Chicago win a huge contract from the U.S. Treasury to serve as financial agent for the Electronic Federal Tax Payments System.[3]

"AT&T delivered a core competency in data and voice networks and the capacity to handle call volumes at an unprecedented scale," Hollis enthusiastically notes. Clearly, AT&T Solutions was not Rodney Dangerfield to the financial services industry. Why was this fledgling IT outsourcer gaining banks' particular respect?

"The financial services sector was really becoming dependent on networks," Rick says, "not just as internal tools, but as go-to-market tools. If you were a bank, you weren't going to do home banking without a robust network with which to connect customers. Also, reliability was a crucial factor for financial services. We could build superior networks because we knew how to design them, build them, and implement them. Plus, we accessed the AT&T network, one of the most reliable networks in the world."

What Rick cites here is all the "noun" stuff—networking's physical nuts and bolts. But it was the "verb" of networking that banks really appreciated: the promise, objectives, and strategy for creating financial value, followed by the action, delivery, and results.

Banks' "merchandise," after all, is money—not a hard good, but symbolic paper, or an account statement's promise of paper, that itself is valueless without a gold reserve. Money, you could say, is a dream—believing in the bank's strength and stability makes the dream come true.

The banks' customers held the belief, and AT&T Solutions did too. It thereby aligned its own strategies and services with the banks' visions and goals. Instead of pitching its services in traditional vendor style by saying "Here's what we can do for you," it said, "Here's what we can do together." Instead of handing down expertise from on high, AT&T Solutions walked a mile—and then the extra mile—in the client banks' shoes, leaving behind any realm of wishful thinking, and entering a promised land of profitably shared belief.

AT&T Solutions Regional Managing Partner Bob Scheier says, "At first, outsourcing was a new concept to many banks, so we had to let them know how our business added value to theirs. We had to make a compelling business case. If we'd just said, 'Hey, we're great guys, and we have super ideas,' but couldn't prove why we were better than other outsourcers, there would have been no case."

AT&T Solutions' work with banks was getting boffo reviews, but how would its act play in other industries? As 1995 came to an end, the stage was set at McDermott International for them to find out.

McDermott is a $3 billion diversified energy services company involved in power generation systems and marine construction. With over 50 locations and 24,000 employees, the corporation serves the U.S. Navy, as well as electrical utilities and oil and gas companies worldwide.

In 1995, McDermott was experiencing a power failure. Its intra-business communications and communications with clients, vendors, suppliers, and partners were being conducted on an international network which, though suited to the company's 1980s mainframe style of computing, was insufficiently responsive to current needs. The company's employees were experiencing e-mail delays of between two days and two weeks, primarily due to the incompatibility of the systems at McDermott's four divisions. Accordingly, McDermott decided that to become more competitive, both now and in the next century, it had to do the following:

1. Migrate to a sophisticated, robust, bandwidth-on-demand voice, data, and video enterprise network infrastructure
2. Focus on its core competencies, expand the business, and reduce operating costs by outsourcing noncore processes[4]

Since installing and managing a new network infrastructure was a noncore process, McDermott shopped around for an outsourcer whose core business was networking.

After auditioning the major players in the outsourcing field, it tapped AT&T Solutions for the job.

A visit to AT&T Solutions' brand-new state-of-the-art Global Client Support Center in Raleigh-Durham, North Carolina (see Exhibit 4), clinched the decision.[5]

AT&T Solutions presents its Global Client Support Center (GCSC) as follows:

AT&T SOLUTIONS GLOBAL CLIENT SUPPORT CENTER

The people, the technology platform, the tools, and the processes at work in the GCSC become a virtual extension of your business—to provide comprehensive proactive and predictive networking management services customized to your company's unique needs.

It's where AT&T Solutions actually delivers its unique ground level, day-to-day value in Networking—a network that gives your business a strategic and tactical edge in the marketplace.

The GCSC keeps you connected to clients, suppliers, and employees, virtually anywhere in the world. This globally linked capability is regionally distributed in four primary locations: Raleigh-Durham, North Carolina; Dublin, Ohio; Reddich, UK; and

Exhibit 4 The Global Client Support Center in Raleigh-Durham, North Carolina

Singapore. Extensions of these facilities exist at key strategic sites in Florida, Canada, Amsterdam, India, and Shanghai. This worldwide, distributed approach allows the GCSC optimum flexibility to address your networking needs anytime, anywhere.

GCSC: People Who Can Move Mountains—A Team That Understands "Mission-Critical"

Since each client's strategy and network architecture is unique, the GCSC assembles teams of networking professionals to manage the client's infrastructure. Our resources are applied based on the nature of the client's agreement, ranging from designated teams for more expansive contracts, to smaller teams managing multiple clients. In short, whatever your requirements may be, we will structure our GCSC teams to your needs. Through the sophisticated technology platform of the GCSC, your team will always have a complete view of your network infrastructure, showing the status and performance of all resources. Depending on the situation, your team can view your network at multiple levels of detail, from individual locations to the global enterprise.

Beyond Skills

The GCSC is a Networking Management Center, not simply a Tier I Help Desk. The Difference lies in the fact that the skill levels of the GCSC associates are much greater than the skill set required to staff a standard Help Desk. Associates at the GCSC are not answering calls regarding word processing programs or desktop-specific issues.

Instead, they are focused on managing more complex issues such as LAN/WAN, server, voice, or application problems. Sophisticated tools identify problems and alert GCSC associates, who immediately notify clients and work with them to isolate and resolve problems. GCSC professionals are trained to "own" all client questions or problems. This includes providing assistance to end users regardless of whether the issue is AT&T's "responsibility" or "not in the scope of the contract." GCSC associates are dedicated to ensuring that the problems are resolved to the client's satisfaction.

Leading Edge Technology and Custom Tools—GEMS: The Global Enterprise Management System

To deliver the service levels your business requires, AT&T Labs has developed a sophisticated networking management system. This highly flexible environment allows the GCSC to support a wide variety of client platforms and technologies and seamlessly manage networks that incorporate equipment and services from multiple vendors. We use best-of-breed management applications from a variety of vendors, including Hewlett-Packard, Cisco, Bay Networks, Cabletron, Microsoft, and Lucent, among others. The key is a single, unified database. This database, continually updated, manually and electronically, allows the GCSC to integrate all of the following clients' functions:

- Management of networking devices
- Electronic gateways and interfaces to AT&T Frame Relay, Software Defined Network, Virtual Telecommunications Network Service, Wireless, and other core capabilities and services
- Asset/Inventory Management
- Service Level Reports
- Moves/Adds/Changes
- Billing

A Window into Your Network

With the main networking management system, your GCSC team can instantly retrieve on-screen "maps" of your entire network, localized and detailed maps showing specific areas, and even individual devices, applications, or users. With this real-time picture at their fingertips, they have the unique ability to monitor and analyze the activity at virtually any point in the network, with a watchful eye on anticipating and preventing problems before they occur.

A Unified Database

At the GCSC, virtually all data about your network is captured and maintained in a single integrated database. This database allows us to coordinate all of your asset, configuration, fault, and traffic data, across all devices and services, speeding trouble resolution, reconfigurations, and other tasks that may involve multiple services and hardware elements. Any changes made to your network are immediately available to all GCSC team members. This holistic view of the network allows for advanced root cause analysis and automated response. If a difficulty is traced to a particular network router, for example, the database can tell your GCSC team the exact physical location of the device, serial number, and model number, and specify a vendor and client contract to arrange a repair or replacement.

Not Only Proactive, but Predictive

The network technology platform at the GCSC is designed to manage your network proactively. Our systems continually monitor your network for even the smallest problems and difficulties, and report them to your team automatically. Often, your GCSC team can notify you or your on-site team that a difficulty was detected, even before anyone noticed or reported a problem. With such early warnings, it is often possible to work around the problem while it is being resolved, and spare your end users any interruption in service. The GCSC systems are designed to collect and report historic fault data and long-term traffic trends. This information can help us determine where problems might occur in the future, and take steps to prevent them in the first place. In addition, your team is so familiar with your network and business that they will suggest valuable improvements and additional services that could avoid potential problems in the future, and thereby greatly improve the performance of your network.

"AT&T Solutions offered the best cost proposal and professional and technical expertise to manage our network, to do the frame-relay conversion, and to provide ongoing network and management support," states John Ruckert, McDermott's vice president of information technology.

Hopes were high at AT&T Solutions for a hit opening at McDermott, and a long and profitable run.

So, after the initial phase of work, what did the critics at McDermott say?

"They beat the living hell out of us," says Rick. "They just said you're doing everything wrong, and if you don't shape up, you're out."

There's no business like show business, it is said.

Could this show be saved? Could the AT&T Solutions cast and crew avoid being run out of town? Would this drama become a real-life tragedy? Could a happy ending be devised in midperformance? Was there a networking-centric script doctor in the house?

And there was another crucial question that AT&T Solutions was posing to itself: Was sticking it out with McDermott financially worthwhile?

"It was a very small deal, around $2 million a year," explains Rick. "Our payroll at the Global Client Support Center alone was bigger than that. We'd just built and equipped that facility, we'd spent $10 million on the platform, and now we were taking hell from McDermott—getting killed, really—for a couple hundred thousand dollars a month. Some people on our team were seriously saying we should bail out."

Rick listened to these team members, while staying tuned to the client's complaints. He didn't prod McDermott to accept the correctness of AT&T Solutions' procedures, and abjured a "my way or the highway" approach. Recalling his own dictum, "The more power you give away, the more powerful you will become," he addressed the problem issues in a "networking-centric" spirit, acting as a listening medium himself and granting equal value to others' points of view.

Would this flexible and generous attitude pay off? Or would the McDermott experience end up as a write-off—a bad trip down a dead-end street?

While the answer hung in the balance, an even larger project with MasterCard came up.

In 1996, MasterCard was supporting 23,000 financial institutions and 325,000 ATMs in 87 countries, and by year's end would process more than six billion transactions. Its existing network boasted uptime of over 99.99 percent. Average transaction time—from point-of-purchase to the retailer's bank to the cardholder's bank and back again—was less than two seconds.[6]

Cardholders and member banks alike were quite happy with the network's present performance, but MasterCard wasn't satisfied.

Why not? Why didn't "if it ain't broke, don't fix it" apply in this case?

"We had a highly redundant and reliable X.25 network, which featured a unique configuration of fully meshed circuit-switched leased lines surrounding our packet-switched backbone," explains Arthur Ahrens, MasterCard's senior vice president of operations services. "In addition to being very sophisticated," he continues, "it was also a capital-intensive operation that couldn't support multiple services efficiently. Also, every year we would incur significant costs to upgrade our network in order to handle the additional load that always occurs during the Thanksgiving-to-Christmas shopping season. Then, in January, the volume would drop off by about 42 percent, and we'd be sitting there with expensive, under-utilized capacity."[7]

MasterCard could have maintained its consumer card market share with some ad hoc upgrades and modifications. Instead, it dreamed of being a leader in the blooming multitrillion-dollar market space of electronic commerce, online shopping, and smart cards. If it could find a technology partner capable of providing an end-to-end networking solution—the nuts-and-bolts hardware plus a guiding, value-driven business plan—then its dream could still come true.

"An open, well-managed, instantly extensible networking platform was vital for MasterCard to take its rightful place in the brave new world of digital money," says Ahrens. "AT&T Solutions stood out as the only business partner qualified to support such a difficult and mission-critical undertaking."

AT&T Solutions promised both the "noun" and the "verb" of networking. And having promised, they delivered.

By moving MasterCard from its old network to a managed Internet Protocol (IP)–based solution, AT&T Solutions enabled the company to shift seamlessly from a capital-intensive networking model to a services-based model, and thus to maximize the value of its financial resources. Seamlessness was critical for MasterCard's nonstop stream of consumer transactions. "The last thing you want is for a merchant or a customer to be frustrated by a communications delay," says Ahrens. "They'll just pull out another card."

The new network also provided distance-insensitive pricing, immediate availability of new technologies, and bandwidth-on-demand. It reduced transaction time by 50 percent, which lowered member banks' costs. Also, the new network was "scalable," meaning that initial baseline capacity could be augmented during peak holiday shopping periods.

The challenge of transitioning MasterCard from a redundant leased-line infrastructure to a new "Virtual Private Network," as well as supporting applications over both the legacy and new networks, was daunting, to say the least. "But," says Ahrens, "AT&T Solutions pulled it off without a hitch."

The McDermott project, though, was still not hitch-free, but the AT&T Solutions team kept listening and working and trying to make things right.

"They were the only client we had so far in our Global Client Support Center, and we were desperate to keep them," recalls Rick. "We were working with our other clients at their own sites, but we were aiming to serve all future clients at our own GCSC."

As the McDermott bridge to the future swayed and threatened to collapse, Rick stayed cool and kept his head up.

"I loved the McDermott experience," he states, "because they were so demanding of us, so tough. They knew what they wanted, and they told us in no uncertain terms. For us it was a crash course in what our Global Client Support Center should be. We listened and learned, and by the end of the course, we passed the test."

With honors, in fact.

In the end, AT&T Solutions met all contracted service levels, lowering McDermott's voice and data WAN management costs by 20 percent, and installing all new technology with no significant capital outlay on the client's part. As the single global WAN provider, AT&T Solutions enabled McDermott to focus on projects it might otherwise have neglected, and thereby to enrich its core business competencies.

McDermott VP John Ruckert says quite simply, "We view our relationship with AT&T Solutions as a complete success."

"McDermott was a much smaller job than MasterCard," says Rick, "but it gave us knowledge and experience beyond any price. The journey we took with McDermott led us to our first real opportunity for a megadeal with Merrill Lynch."

"Merrill Lynch? You think you'll win that contract? Don't hold your breath."

That's basically what the rest of AT&T said to AT&T Solutions. (Telling AT&T Solutions they can't do something, though, is the way to ensure they get it done.)

At the time Merrill Lynch was running its own global data transmission network, leasing bare-bones capacity from MCI and operating it with a nearly 100-member in-house staff. AT&T had tried three times in 10 years for Merrill's network account, but each time MCI had held it with a lower bid.

Having already suffered through many such AT&T-instigated delays, Merrill's CIO Howard Shallcross was fed up. "There was no willingness to negotiate in good faith," he states, "no spirit of compromise. No one from a higher level in AT&T came in to tell these lawyers to take a hike. They just didn't seem to want the business."

So what did Shallcross do?

He stood up, declared the deal dead, and walked away.

"AT&T was used to dictating the terms of its contracts," he says, "whereas MCI came in and said to us, 'What terms and conditions do you want?' And within a day they had the deal."

Leasing MCI capacity and operating it in-house worked for Merrill until the bull market 1990s fattened the firm and made its communications needs far more complex. Merrill's IT staff began complaining that it was overburdened and couldn't accomplish its work.

On February 7, 1995, two of Merrill's technology chiefs came to the firm's executive vice president for operations, Edward L. Goldberg, and said this:

> **Merrill Lynch is a financial services company, not a telecommunications company.**
> **Merrill Lynch should focus on its core business.**
> **Merrill Lynch needs an outside specialist firm to handle its network.**

Goldberg's response: "What took you so long to tell me this?"

AT&T, MCI, and the Sprint Corporation all bid for the Merrill account. (Other telecommunications carriers shied from the challenge, intimidated by the prospect of managing a network of Merrill's huge size and scope.)[8]

"It was the biggest, most complex deal we'd gone after yet," says Rick. "We wanted it, we needed it, and we had to win."

That's when the AT&T naysayers chimed in: "It's a nonstarter," they said. "A dead end."

Did the naysayers bother the AT&T Solutions team?

"I call them ankle biters," Rick says. "If you look down and respond to every nip around your feet, you'll lose your forward vision and never take a step."

But don't ankle biters deserve a good, swift kick?

"They weren't acting maliciously. They didn't want us to fail. They just thought we were straying from the well-beaten corporate path. Which we were, of course."

What bothered them the most?

"Pooling people from different areas to handle engagements—it drove them nuts. Having people working on several engagements led by different partners at once so each person had more than one boss. We were following the Andersen Consulting management model, which could flex. But AT&T, like most big corporations, is like the military. It's structured hierarchically, in levels, so a manager can say, 'These are my people. This is my team.'" Our new model confused them. It scared them to death. They said it wouldn't work." (See Exhibit 5.)

But Rick had belief.

"To tell you the truth, even some of our own people were confused by the model at first, especially the ones who came out of IBM. However, Victor Millar, AT&T Solutions' first CEO, had been the head of Andersen, and understood the model intimately. He brought some Andersen people with him and they really helped us understand it and make it work. So what our ankle biters saw as our great weakness, we saw as our great strength."

Not all of AT&T was skeptical, however. Rick had believers where it counted the most: at the top.

"We were fortunate that President Alex Mandl and Chairman and CEO Bob Allen and his operating leadership team had faith in us. 'Go for it,' they said. 'Give it a shot.' That gave us air cover."

The truth is, the AT&T Solutions team liked being an "orphan" at AT&T. "In a way it was easier," Rick says, "because without a huge base, we didn't have a lot to lose. We could move faster because we didn't have to ask for permission at every step. We were creating the market as

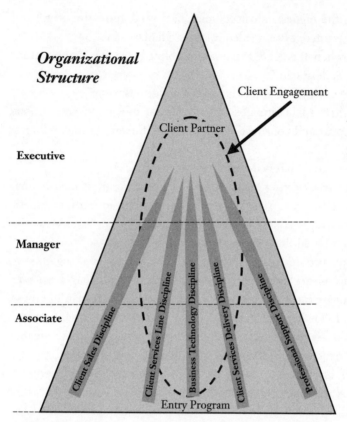

Exhibit 5 The Organizational Structure of a Client Engagement

much as meeting it, believing in our clients as we made them believe in us. And the fact is, we wanted AT&T to believe something, too: that we could come out of nowhere—the conference room, in this case—and make some dents. We could put together a bigger and better business than anyone thought we could."

Merrill Lynch would be a big dent, indeed.

"Without doubt, Merrill Lynch would be a watershed for us," affirms Rick. "We needed marquee accounts, and Merrill was as big as they come. A client of that size and stature would finally establish who we were, both to ourselves and to the marketplace. It would give us clout. Our sales force would be walking about half a foot taller on the street. 'We just won Merrill Lynch,' they'd say to new prospective clients, 'so you might want to talk to us.'"

The talk, meanwhile, was about winning the Merrill Lynch contract in the first place—and here the old catch-22 reared its head: How could AT&T Solutions, in its first full year of operation, present itself as large and experienced and smart enough to redesign, implement, and manage a network as big and complex as the Merrill Lynch network?

"A lot of AT&T people thought I was nuts," laughs Rick. "They said, 'How can you be making these wild claims about all the stuff you can do, and all the stuff you're going to do, and how big you are, when you're not that big yet?'"

But the AT&T Solutions team wasn't making wild claims; they weren't shooting from the hip. "We didn't go in there promising the world," Rick asserts. "How could we do that? We didn't know what Merrill wanted. So we listened and listened, and listened some more, and we found out what they wanted."

Bruce Sieben was one of the Merrill technology chiefs who originally urged the company to outsource its network. As he recalls, "Some other companies said to us, 'We can run your network for 2.9 cents a minute and do everything you want.'"

But promises are just talk, and talk is cheap.

"It's the easiest thing in the world to open up a telecommunications business," says Sieben. "You buy some switches. You buy some remote access equipment. But the difference between AT&T and XYZ was that AT&T had a service and support engine and a serve-and-support culture, and XYZ didn't."

Merrill's Executive VP Edward Goldberg says the firm's ultimate choice was clear-cut. "We felt that we wanted the expertise, the know-how, and the discipline of AT&T Solutions," he states.

But would Merrill put up with the old arrogant, nitpicking AT&T style of contract negotiation?

They didn't have to, as it turned out.

HOWARD SHALLCROSS'S STORY: AN EARLY CLIENT'S VIEW

With Rick Roscitt at the table, the difference was like night and day. He didn't dictate terms. He engaged us in a good faith give-and-take. He didn't follow internal rules of engagement. He based his trust on a handshake and a mutual willingness to bend and flex to get the deal and the job done.

Every time we hit a snag, and his lawyers balked, Rick insisted on working out the problem on the spot. He said he'd take the risk. And he was hungry. His start-up enterprise needed customers to get launched. Merrill would be a flagship account. He took an entrepreneurial approach, and so we did the transaction on businessmen's terms, not lawyers' terms. And he was honest, a man of his word, and courageous, and I'll only work with a partner like that.

Of course, the lawyers played their part. They had to, because each company had such tremendous liabilities—management, legal, and all that. The contract had to protect the shareholders, as it always does. Beyond that, though, we agreed we weren't going to be slaves to that document, and we wouldn't refer to it again and again. So we put it in the drawer and left it and got on with our work. A partnership can't evolve and succeed if it's hung up every minute on legal points.

I use the word *partnership* because that's what I felt this should be. I wasn't just looking for a new vendor, I didn't just want to buy new boxes from IBM, and I couldn't keep upgrading our personnel. I needed help reengineering our network, help in changing Merrill from being reactive in technology to being proactive and seizing the day. We needed a cultural change. We needed end-to-end solutions so our business could advance. And AT&T really got into that. They shared our vision. They got as excited as we were about making this work. They saw what was in it for both sides, knowing it wouldn't always be a 50/50 split. Sometimes it would be 70/30 or 40/60, depending on economic conditions of the moment and where the industry was. But it would always be evenly balanced in terms of working toward the same goal.

Partnering is tough, but the payoffs are great. They're not promised in the contract, but they're out there, like the carrot on the stick. What earns the rewards are the dollars and cents, the resources, the policies and procedures, and the cultures that each partner puts to work.

I know Rick was under big pressure. He had to make this a profitable account. For our part, we had to lower our costs. These were life-and-death business issues that we couldn't turn over to subordinates. As leaders, we had to address them ourselves. So we shook hands, and we did just that.

Edward Goldberg had been impressed by AT&T's disciplined approach to this engagement. This discipline was partly motivated—indeed self-enforced—by a compensation schedule keyed to the performance and reliability of the network, and adjustable on a sliding scale that became more demanding over time. Discipline, however, did not preclude flexibility—which was fortunate because the central network technology changed radically between AT&T Solutions' winning the contract in January 1996 and signing it in May.

In January, the technology included computerized switches made by Cisco Systems called "routers" and "hubs." That winter, Cisco introduced an improved hybrid router and hub called a "rub."[9] Being just one box instead of two, the new design appealed to Merrill Lynch because, with their 700 leased locations in the United States, there was a premium on space. Although the new component was immediately available, AT&T Solutions had to customize, install, and test it for specific Merrill Lynch use. Could this work be accomplished by spring? Since AT&T Solutions was part of AT&T, its nimbleness, to many observers, was in doubt.

Those observers should have observed more closely: Though AT&T and AT&T Solutions were joined at the hip, each marched to a far different beat.

"AT&T Solutions was basically like a start-up company," says Howard Shallcross. "They showed that they could adapt."

"We had to be quick-change artists," comments Rick, "and we had to morph. It just shows how fast the changes come in this business, not just from one engagement to the next, but within a single job. If you're not nimble, if you can't make decisions quickly and turn on a dime, you're cooked."

With the contract signed, and the technology issues sorted out, who would be the general manager for the Merrill account?

Fresh from his success at Chase Manhattan, Gerry Pape was picked.

GERRY PAPE'S STORY, PART 2: MERRILL LYNCH

Being located in New York, Merrill Lynch was like Chase, only more so. The culture was even more intense. Merrill was our biggest deal yet, and it was off to a rocky start.

The situation was this: Merrill's existing network had grown out of control. Their volumes were skyrocketing. These were data networks that hadn't been designed to deal with such big volumes. Plus, they were breaking because they either hadn't been installed correctly or hadn't been built right.

That's what I walked into. This was in-your-face New York on a bad day. It was pretty ugly, to tell the truth. I couldn't let it rattle me, though. We had a job to do. And after Chase, I felt pretty confident. By the time I left Chase, by the way, we had PCs and laptops, desks, telephones, the works. Even pencils with our own names on them!

But Merrill was a whole new game. These were global networks, 24 hours a day, so our job was round-the-clock, too. Merrill was basically making its brokers into financial consultants, and our networking platform was intended to let them do that.

Most of our equipment was from Cisco. We'd meet with them and the Merrill people three times a day at 10, 2, and 4—the "Dr. Pepper meetings," we called them—just to check in with each other on what needed replacing and what needed to be fixed.

We worked both short-term and long-term. Short-term was anything from today to six months. Long-term was…I'm not sure we ever got to long-term. In theory, long-term was six months to two years.

On top of the technology, we had a business to run—financials and P&Ls—plus, we were managing all the staff. It was a thrill, to say the least. Never a dull day. But we got through it. In fact, we got very close. I became part of Howard Shallcross's technology team. I worked hand-in-hand with his data center guy and his desktop guy and all his staff. I went to all of Howard's staff meetings every week. I was an outsider and an insider all at once. They used to joke that as an insider, I could take some of the credit for things that went right, and as an outsider, I could be blamed for what went wrong.

In the end, a GM's rapport with the client's management team is the key to making the whole relationship work. The trust has to be established early and developed over time. I'm the advocate for the client inside AT&T. Many times the client's goals differ from those of my own company, but I have to fight for them, even though I'm paid by AT&T. I'm sometimes accused of being on the payroll of the wrong company. I take that as a compliment. My bias is to err on the client's side, because no one else will do it if I don't. And no one can do it as well.

Merrill was exciting, no doubt about that. Their culture is wound up so tight. It's based on making trades fast, because if a stock is selling right now at $60, it could go down to $59 or up to $61 in two seconds flat. It's a crapshoot either way. Speed is everything. Sometimes it's the only thing, and sometimes that's not good for Merrill Lynch. Here's what I mean by that:

Howard Shallcross invited Rick to come and talk at a meeting of the 80 or 90 top managers who run all the technology for Merrill Lynch. It was down at a resort in Atlantic City, and Rick flew in to give his speech. And he was superb. He's great in situations like that. Well, Rick finished his presentation and asked for questions, and somebody asked, "Well, Rick, we've always told you what's wrong with AT&T. Now why don't you tell us how we can improve? What's wrong with Merrill Lynch?"

Rick didn't flinch. His response was that Merrill might give more time and attention to planning and making decisions where technology was concerned. In short, Merrill should put the words "ready" and "aim" in front of "fire."

That hit the audience right where they lived. Because they all knew they were weak on that. Then Rick said that new technology doesn't solve problems overnight. One new box in one new location won't do the trick. You have to think it through, plan it all out, integrate it, and give it sufficient time to work. Both your users' and your customers' needs must be taken into account.

From a general manager's perspective, it's a serious issue, make no mistake. As outsourcers we have to develop an architecture that defines and guides the whole transformation process. Otherwise, some clients go into the equipment room and start plugging in this and that and they make a mess. Since it's a shared network, everyone feels the damage when they do that. And then they blame us for managing the network badly. They say they were never anywhere near the equipment room. You want to give them a piece of your mind, but, at the same time, you don't want to antagonize them and lose their support. These engagements aren't just about technology. They're about people, too, and a general manager has to be sensitive to that.

On the subject of people, 75 Merrill Lynch technology specialists were made employees of AT&T, though they stayed at the Merrill offices. Although there was no change in their actual work, they were suddenly viewed by some of their Merrill coworkers as being in a distinct AT&T camp. As a result, they were offered little help. Howard Shallcross had to remind the Merrill people that they were all working to promote Merrill Lynch, regardless of which company wrote their checks.

Except for that instance, however, a spirit of true collaboration was maintained as the project progressed, much to Shallcross's delight. He was accustomed to more adversarial vendor-client relationships in which the parties played their cards close to the vest. Rather than anticipate problems and work cooperatively to head them off, he was accustomed to seeing one company wait for the other to trip and fall. At any bobble by either side, the contract would be whipped out, accusations hurled, and the legal staffs wrangling to settle the dispute.

Shallcross was tired of that. For one thing, the brokerage business was too fast-paced for legal squabbles. If the network was down, it had to be fixed immediately so business was not lost. A fine-tooth comb review of the contract could wait.

When cost issues arose, Rick and Shallcross often shared financials to align goals with resources. Each said to the other, in effect, "I want you to make money, but this partnership won't make sense unless I make money too. So let's see where each of us stands right now, and where each of us wants to go."

For certain, this was far beyond the usual vendor-client relationship.

As a marquee client for AT&T Solutions, Merrill was of great value in landing more accounts, and Howard Shallcross was glad to be a reference as well as a facilitator for the AT&T Solutions team. When one potential AT&T Solutions client complained to Howard about the AT&T lawyers' overbearing approach, Howard told Rick, who promptly flew to the site of the negotiations and got the discussion back on track.

AT&T Solutions was creating its own business entity—a start-up corporate culture—that was light on its feet.

AT&T Solutions was marching in double- and triple-time at the speed of change.

Since the extraordinary pace of change in outsourcing is a product of both the technology and the clients it serves, they had no choice.

"You think you're moving fast but the customers are moving just as fast," observes Rick, "so it's hard to gain any ground. Everybody wants everything in real-time. They're too busy to wait. If they don't get what they want when they want it, they go to someone else. It's all about speed, which these days is cultural. At some point, though, businesses can't run any faster, so they've got to run smarter. Networking is what lets them do that."

Networking as both noun and verb. Networking as both subject and ACTION.

"It's cultural," Rick repeats, "which means it's strategy and implementation, bricks and clicks—but also the mind and the heart."

But why is it cultural? And what is culture, anyway?

Why is "To be or not to be" a philosophical quandary to some companies, and to others, a clarion call to arms?

Why do some enterprises of great pitch and moment lose the name of action, while others infuse their dreams with the native hue of resolution, and live to dream another day?

Chapter 5 addresses these questions. Since time waits for no one in the new economy, you'll want to be nimble about turning the page. Before it's too late.

DEBRIEFING

Customer Intimacy

In Chapter 2 networking is described in terms of noun and verb:

> The noun was the network's physical infrastructures. The verb was what one did with those infrastructures to create and sustain business value.
>
> The noun was talk. The verb was action.
>
> The noun was the promise. The verb was the delivery and the results.
>
> The noun was investment. The verb was design, strategy, and execution.
>
> The noun was wishful thinking. The verb was a value-driven business plan. "A plan that's not driven by value can't produce value," as Rick said.

Value, of course, had to be realized by AT&T Solutions and its customers alike—and it certainly was realized with Chase Manhattan

Bank. This relationship was as much a partnership as a vendor-client pact. The same was true with AT&T Solutions' relationships with other banks, as well as with companies in other industries such as McDermott International, MasterCard, and Merrill Lynch.

In these relationships, AT&T Solutions became more than customer-centric. It became customer-intimate, in fact.

How do we define and apply the concept of customer intimacy? Like Rick, we see it in terms of noun and verb.

The Noun

A topic this sensitive demands total accuracy, so we'll call on *The Random House College Dictionary* again for help:

> **intimacy, n., 1. a close, familiar, and usually affectionate or loving personal relationship. 2. a detailed knowledge or deep understanding of a place, subject, period of history.**

Should companies really be intimate like this with their customers? You bet.

Old companies certainly were not. Their method of romancing customers involved the following:

• Conducting market research
• Developing a product labeled "One Size Fits All"
• Market testing the product to death
• Manufacturing the product in large quantities
• Rolling out the product

This approach was slow and, despite all the market research and testing, kept customers at a distance. That is, it viewed customers as targets that the product was aimed to hit.

This ready-aim-fire strategy offered attractive features to satisfy buyers' product-specific needs, but didn't suggest how the product would work within a system of products. Thus, it didn't address, or solve, problems end-to-end.

Customer-focused this approach may have been. Customer-intimate it was not.

Traditional companies such as the pre-1990s AT&T regarded the marketplace as a shop for hawking wares, not a forum where customers could be engaged in a discussion of their deepest dreams and needs. No wonder that few close, familiar, or affectionate relationships developed. How could they develop while products were still just hard-good nouns—commodities, in fact? Only by featuring personal expertise could selling be de-commoditized. Only by hot-wiring product nouns with problem-solving verbs could companies distinguish themselves from their competition by helping customers not just to acquire essential articles but also to realize their dreams.

Customer intimacy is a tango, and the promise of networking solutions was Rick's invitation to the dance. As the music began, his card filled up—as did the ballroom floor with other networking outsourcers, all of them promising customer intimacy, too.

Suddenly, in the new-economy marketplace, the air was filled with romance.

The Verbs

Define Customer Problems

Every engagement has two phases, says Bob Heinz, AT&T Solutions' client engagement manager. In the first phase—Transition—AT&T Solutions researches the client's current way of doing business, down to the last relevant detail. Then the problem situation is rigorously examined and analyzed, and the range of corrective actions is reviewed. Finally, the best problem-solving approach is affirmed, based on its promise of optimizing value and cutting costs. The actual work procedures are then defined and sequenced, enabling the second phase—Transformation—to begin.

Transition and Transformation.
Understanding the problem before attacking it.
Learning to walk before you run.

Create Solutions That Add Value

Why offer "like for like for less" when you can proudly and more profitably provide "best in class," and thus raise your customers to the level of the "best of the best"?

Optimize, don't commoditize.

Help your customers—and your own enterprise—to break away from the pack.

Fire Impossible Customers

As we've said, customer intimacy is a tango. Some customers don't dance very well, though. Some can't, or won't, dance at all.

Drop them. You can't dance till dawn with a customer who is a soloist by nature, or with one who has two left feet. There are plenty of other willing customer-partners still out there just waiting to pair up with you.

Make Your Whole Team Customer-Intimate

The customer intimacy dance is not just a managers' ball. All teams and team members from both companies must join in. Instead of Fred Astaire and Ginger Rogers in a spotlight, think of a conga line or a Virginia reel.

Measure, Measure, Measure

Perform this simple two-step to make everyone accountable for his or her performance, and fully committed to achieving top results:

1. Prepare a simple monthly summary of results and give it to everyone on the team. Include financial tallies, plus gauges of team and customer satisfaction.
2. Discuss the results with the team and determine whatever corrections should be made.

5

Building a Winning Culture

If we specify that we are talking about excellence in business arts, let-ters, manners, and so on, and about a form or stage of business civiliza-tion, we can apply the following definition from *The Random House College Dictionary* to the corporate world.

> **culture, n. 1. the quality in a person or society that arises from an interest in and acquaintance with excellence in arts, letters, manners, scholarly pursuits, etc. 2. a particular form or stage of civilization.**

The dictionary has more to say about culture. It is also

3. the sum total of ways of living built up by a group of human beings and transmitted from one generation to another.

Since a company's culture inspires and informs actions at all levels and over time, this definition can also be applied to the corporate world.

Culture can also mean

4. development or improvement of the mind by education or training.

Education and training play a huge part in creating, developing, inculcating, and propagating corporate culture, as we shall see later.

Finally, culture can signify

5. the growth resulting from the cultivation of microorganisms as bacteria, or of tissues, for scientific study, medicinal use, etc.

Recalling the retiring AT&T executive who told Rick, "The corporate body treats new things like foreign substances and tries to expel them," we can even apply the biological definition of culture to corporate "microorganisms" and "tissues."

Rick's view on culture is this: "On the one hand, it can be a sort of soft, gooey, indefinable mystique based on heroes, legends, and icons. At Federal Express, for instance, they tell stories about their founder, Fred Smith. At the end of the stories the storytellers say, 'That's the way Fred likes things done, so we do things his way.' But Fred can't be everywhere in a global company that big; his views on everything can't be known, and yet all of FedEx seems to know what he wants. They're driven by his icon."

Workplace behaviors can be iconic, too.

"There's the Silicon Valley company that knocked off on Fridays at three o'clock and drank beer. These bashes became famous, and the company became a legend for kicking back during work time and having fun. But these things come and go. The odds are that company is back to the corporate nine-to-five-or-later and their Fridays are alcohol-free."

What's the other type of culture?

"The one based on commitment to customer satisfaction, employee enjoyment, and success. Stories and legends are fine, but if that's all a company has for motivation, then it's hollow at the core."

But beyond these generic definitions of culture, what is the AT&T Solutions culture per se? Can a few words accurately depict what Rick says is equal parts strategy, implementation, bricks, and clicks—as well as the mind and heart?

No, a few words can't. But a look at some key events that shaped AT&T Solutions' culture will illustrate the development and ultimate essence of this business unit's corporate soul.

"I was waiting to catch a flight," says Rick. "I was on my way to make an important presentation to a potential client, and the fellow from AT&T Solutions who was bringing me my briefing packet hadn't shown up."

Rick asked the gate attendant when the boarding gate would be closed. "In about two minutes," the attendant said.

"Then my man rushed up, sweating and out of breath, and handed me the materials. I blasted him for being so late. I really chewed him out."

The breathless colleague explained his tardiness: he had to run around to nine different AT&T buildings to gather the briefing sheets.

Why nine buildings? Because AT&T Solutions, in its rapid growth, had been taking space wherever AT&T had it available, which was all over the map.

"Sorry," Rick said to his colleague as he showed his ticket at the gate. "I understand, it wasn't your fault."

In his seat on the plane, Rick reflected on how a business enterprise suffered by being so far-flung:

It couldn't collect materials from multiple locations without wasting valuable time.

It couldn't easily gather people together for meetings.

It couldn't establish a sense of physical, intellectual, and emotional togetherness, and thus it was hampered in generating collective spirit and morale.

"We needed our own building," Rick recalled concluding as his jet took off. "I realized that we'd never forge our own identity and we'd never develop our own AT&T Solutions culture until we all had the same roof over our heads."

What kind of building would it be, though?

"It had to be *us*," says Rick. "By that I mean it had to reflect who we were in terms of our self-image and our image to the world. And it had to add to who we were in terms of business value. A new building would be a value proposition in itself."

AT&T offered two floors in one of its existing buildings. Rick said no thanks.

"We'd have had our own space, but we'd have been neighbors with big AT&T. We'd have met them in the cafeteria, and it wouldn't have been hostile, but we'd have been seen as a little crazy with our different structure, different titles, different approach to the clock—I mean, we had people logging 48 straight hours, catnapping at their desks, spending six weekends in a row at their desks."

"AT&T took offense when we turned them down," recalls Rick. "It was like parents asking their kids who just got out of college to keep on living at home. But we just couldn't stay with them. We had to make the break."

So Rick went to real estate firms and told them what he needed:

- A building apart from any other AT&T location
- 100,000 square feet of space for a start
- A cost of under $14 per square foot
- A campus environment to accommodate future expansion
- No other current tenants, so that AT&T Solutions would have the whole space to itself

The real estate agents scanned Rick's criteria and said, "Dream on, you can't get all that." They took him around to see available properties to prove that they were right.

Then a friend of Rick's mentioned a set of unoccupied buildings in Florham Park, New Jersey—a million square feet built on spec 10 years before for Blue Cross/Blue Shield, which had subsequently abandoned the building. Now the buildings were available through the receiver for a net price of just what Rick wanted—around $14 per square foot.

Rick jumped at the opportunity.

Acquiring the space, though, was just a start. Now the interiors would need to be gutted and customized to support the AT&T Solutions enterprise in every possible way.

Rather than design by decree, Rick had ergonomics experts ask all the functional groups what they needed to work at their peak.

What they needed most, it turned out, were good rooms in which to meet—and enough of them so groups didn't have to reserve the rooms three months in advance (and so meetings didn't have to break up after one hour to let the next group come in). Also, the rooms would have to have more than one telephone wall jack so the 20 laptop users wouldn't have to fight to plug their modems in.

Adequate space was important, too. Instead of normal-sized conference suites there would have to be expansive "war rooms" where massive engagements could be plotted on wall maps and charts.

Overall, instead of a traditional "office" environment, AT&T Solutions demanded a combination nerve center, command center, and intellectual playground-gymnasium where its people—individually and collectively—could Dream, Believe, Dare, and Do.

"We looked at the new building as an empowering tool," says Rick, "as opposed to just a place to be."

In Rick's other favored terms, the building-as-tool was the "noun" of the enterprise, the physical implement for making and shaping networking solutions. It was the extension of its users' hands and minds to generate mechanical advantage and facilitate action that would profit AT&T Solutions and its clients alike.

In facilitating action, the building-noun was also the subject of the enterprise's "verb," of course.

When the building was ready, the unit's shingle read:

AT&T SOLUTIONS

Just the name of the outsourcing unit. No AT&T corporate globe logo in sight.

"The AT&T logo police hated us for that," shrugs Rick. "But we weren't the globe, just our own part of it, all contained within that building. We felt we should have our own name out front and nothing but."

Says Vice President of Public Relations Jim Byrnes, "AT&T Solutions was founded as a consulting firm, and that was very different in nature from AT&T. Our work was different and so our image—to ourselves and to our customers—had to be, too."

"We didn't want the usual hierarchical job titles," says Rick. "So we called ourselves associates, managers, and partners, which better suited what we were."

Bill Blinn, vice president of human resources, came to AT&T Solutions from AT&T. But AT&T Solutions interviewed him a dozen times before deciding that a corporate fellow could fit in with a start-up professional services firm. Says Blinn, "In every interview I could see them asking themselves, 'Does this guy get it?' I guess I convinced them I did."

Vice President of Marketing Bill O'Brien notes, "The AT&T Solutions culture is undyingly dedicated to results, and people on all levels know this. They also know the financial health of the business, which is better than any other company I've worked for, including AT&T itself. Consequently, everyone feels that they're helping to row the boat."

Are AT&T Solutions people mavericks?

"In most large companies," says O'Brien, "employees follow well-defined processes. At AT&T Solutions, we don't have a rulebook or a set of precedents based on decades of past success. We just say to customers, 'yes, we can do that.' We don't figure something is impossible because we haven't done it before. Every engagement is new. Every client has a different name and face. Each deal is a custom deal. It's an entrepreneurial culture. We like to put the first marks on the ice with our skates."

"We all feel real ownership of the business," says Dick Anderson, AT&T Solutions' current chief technology officer (CTO). "We work hard on our own terms. We say, 'Hold us accountable, give us some space, and let us go.' We're like a dotcom in that regard. And that spirit is spreading throughout AT&T, in part thanks to us."

Perhaps no one knows the AT&T Solutions culture better than Frank Ianna, currently president of AT&T Network Services. Frank was at AT&T when AT&T Solutions was just a dream.

FRANK IANNA'S STORY

AT&T Solutions culture is customer oriented and focused on results. And it's just one of the cultures inside AT&T. There's also the business culture, the AT&T network culture, the cable culture, and the wireless culture.

We acquired wireless in 1994. Put the wireless folks in a conference room and they all pick up their wireless phones. Almost just to let you know who they are. And this has influenced AT&T. Now everyone in the corporation has a wireless phone. Everyone's using wireless voice mail and wireless e-mail. It shows how a new culture can affect the old existing culture after it's brought in.

Our AT&T Solutions culture is a very proud one. We hurt when we fail, not just professionally but personally. We feel a part of what we create, and when it doesn't work or is rejected for whatever reason, we take it very hard because we really care. A failure is a train wreck. "The network is in trouble," we say, like it was one of us.

But while we're proud, we aren't puffed up. There aren't a lot of fancy office trappings here. The office isn't where we pull rank on each other. It's where we work.

Also, we have very good salespeople, and we take pride in that. Many of them are from AT&T Labs, so they know their stuff inside and out. And they're not just technically savvy; they have great people skills, too. Because this is a people business, after all, we're providing personal service, and our customers appreciate how we work. We're flattered that a lot of them have copied our approach. Whenever I look at Merrill Lynch's culture, I see reflections of us. That makes me feel great. I see our all-out dedication, our attitude of respect, and our teamwork.

And our integrity above all else. When we're right, we say so, and when we're wrong, we admit our mistakes. And we correct them quickly. In our teams we can disagree with each other pretty vehemently, we can be screaming one moment and the next we're back to business, and it's all blown away. What doesn't blow away is the basic personal respect. And we know how to laugh; we're very good at that. Rick's very funny, very sharp, and while his humor can be cutting sometimes, it's never disrespectful. It's never meant to hurt.

But there's always a risk of criticism sounding personal, and we guard against that. "It's your *idea*, not you, that I don't like," is how we try to say it—instead of, "Well, I think your idea stinks, Joe. What do you think about it yourself?"

Rick saw AT&T Solutions' new building as both a greenhouse for growing the enterprise and as a secure and stable "home sweet home."

And inside that facility the AT&T Solutions culture took root. Every day they could see more clearly who they were and who they wanted to be. And that gave them confidence, and confidence breeds more confidence, and that's when dreams become belief.

And so they did.

THE WALL STREET JOURNAL

Thursday, August 14, 1997

AT&T NAMES ROSCITT PRESIDENT AND CEO OF CONSULTING UNIT

AT&T Corp. named Richard R. Roscitt president and chief executive officer of AT&T Solutions, a move that is expected to increase the visibility of the two-year-old company.

The telecommunications giant also named Mr. Roscitt, 46 years old, executive vice president of the corporation. In his new role at the consulting unit, Mr. Roscitt succeeds Victor Millar, 62, who assumes new duties as senior advisor to AT&T's operations team.[1]

Julie Meringer, an industry analyst with Forrester Research, saw Rick's elevation as his well-earned reward for building AT&T Solutions from scratch.

"They were a no-show," Meringer said. "He's given them some credibility. He's given them some brand."[2]

AT&T Solutions' more than $4 billion in orders to date certified the credibility; the $2.5 billion more expected by year's end affirmed the brand.

Talk about dreams and belief.

Talk about a culture of rapid-fire success.

"The move now is to get AT&T Solutions out of incubation," Rick told the press. "We want to grow it, and I think with my 25 years at AT&T, the leadership at the top believes that I'm the right guy to do it."

Was this the end of the AT&T–AT&T Solutions cultural rift?

AT&T spokeswoman Joyce Van Duzer said this: "Now that [AT&T Solutions] has proven itself and matured to a certain extent, it made sense to bring it in closer to the fold."

Closer to the fold? Wait a minute, wasn't AT&T Solutions just moments ago leaving home after college and making its own way in the world?

"Increasingly, [AT&T Solutions] is going to become a high-profile and important part of [AT&T's] business," telecom industry analyst

Jeffrey Kagan observed. "It's going to be the centerpiece off of which all their business services will sprout."

Centerpiece? Was AT&T Solutions being sucked back into the belly of the beast? Was it falling out of high-flying orbit and returning to AT&T Mother Earth? Was the AT&T Solutions maverick team abandoning their firebrand, breakaway culture and—God forbid—selling out?

No way. Just the opposite, in fact. Indeed, it was corporate AT&T that was bending in AT&T Solutions' direction, boosting the outsourcer's standing in the marketplace by showing it new respect.

That respect took the form of a job—which meant that instead of hauling its offspring back home to live, parent AT&T was hiring its own overachieving kid.

THE WALL STREET JOURNAL
Thursday, September 10, 1997

AT&T'S SOLUTIONS WILL RUN PARENT'S COMPUTER NETWORK

AT&T Corp. said it will shift the management of its internal computer operations to AT&T Solutions, its network-consulting and computer-outsourcing service, a move that could bolster the two-year-old unit's credibility with clients.[3]

How big was this job?

Very big.

AT&T was assigning AT&T Solutions to manage and maintain its network computing infrastructure (desktops, servers, and LANs), its voice, data, and image networking activities, and its massive mainframe computer operations totaling over 10,000 MIPS of processing power.[4]

It was transferring 5,000 of its own computer-maintenance employees, plus over 2,000 Unix servers, 120,000 desktop computers, and 130 million megabytes of network traffic, to the AT&T Solutions unit.[5]

That's respect.

The respect was mutual: "AT&T is a world-class client," declared Rick, "and we plan to give them world-class service and prices."

And world-class savings, too. AT&T Solutions' centralized IT management figured to save AT&T hundreds of millions of dollars toward its corporate goal of trimming $2.6 billion in costs.

Of course, AT&T was paying AT&T Solutions more than just respect.

"I don't know of any networking contract that's ever been of this scale," said Rick.

What scale was he talking about?

Close to $1 billion a year.

More than that, the contract put AT&T Solutions in a position to compete with the likes of IBM and EDS for other high-level, enterprise network computing engagements. "We won't be going after stand-alone businesses from this point," said Rick. "We're pursuing the very biggest corporations now. We're aiming for the stars."

From launch to deep space engagements in two years—that's quick success. It was no fluke, however, because AT&T Solutions—with its light-of-foot, triple-time, damn-the-torpedoes, action verb–driven, Dream, Believe, Dare, Do culture—was destined for stardom from the start.

"He had a very clear vision," recalls Bill O'Brien, "and though it took awhile for it to take hold, Rick never gave up. I can remember people within AT&T saying, 'Oh, yeah, networking the noun and networking the verb, who cares! We build networks. We know what we do.' And Rick would say, 'We *do* build networks, but it's going to take more than building networks to succeed in the long run.' He was tenacious. He knew he was right. He knew enough about the market and about our company to have the courage of his convictions. And while the naysayers raised their voices all around him, he never—thank God—went off the track."

Still, for all its brash independence, AT&T Solutions' straight-shooting honesty and trustworthiness made it a chip off the AT&T family values cultural block.

"For the sake of our own identity, we kept our distance from big AT&T," says Rick, "but we took the corporate brand name with us when we called on potential clients. It opened doors everywhere we went. People didn't have to know who we were at AT&T Solutions, but they sure knew AT&T. They trusted AT&T, and so they trusted us."

Trust, of course, is built on truthfulness.

Says Dick Anderson, "What inspired me most about Rick was how honest he was about the business. He wouldn't hesitate to say to a client, 'You know, we didn't do this right,' or, 'We don't think we should work for you,' or, 'We should make an adjustment here.' His aim wasn't to smell like a rose all the time but instead to make things right. He instilled in us that if we didn't make mistakes, we weren't trying hard enough. He backed us up and inspired us to do our best work. His leadership was as much logical as motivational. With our talents and vision and courage, it was obvious that we should succeed! That lit a fire in us, but it made us very comfortable, too."

One might say that Rick empowered AT&T Solutions people.

The deal between AT&T and AT&T Solutions showed that two different corporate cultures didn't have to be mutually exclusive or at odds over style and approach. Each could mark its own turf without installing an electrified fence. One culture could learn from the other and employ its services and attributes when it wished. As partners the two might be an odd couple at first—and then become a perfect match.

Could the match, though, survive the executive changes that were currently in the works?

As Rick was appointed AT&T Solutions' president and CEO and Victor Millar was designated senior advisor to the corporate operations team, a search for a new chairperson and CEO of the AT&T corporation was underway.

Rick was very concerned about who that person might be.

"Worst case, it could have been someone who looked at AT&T Solutions and said, 'You're small change, I can't help you, come back when you can prove you'll make some bigger bucks.'"

To believe that Rick's vision was realizable and approve major corporate support, the new CEO would have to make a leap of faith.

To help the CEO make that leap—to make him or her believe that AT&T Solutions could grow at a never-before-achieved rate—Rick would have to face another catch-22.

Unless, that is, the CEO was a fellow dreamer who believed that dreams fueled by daring and doing could come true.

C. Michael Armstrong had been chairman and CEO of Hughes Electronics Corporation for 6 years. Before that he had been at IBM for 30 years, starting as a systems engineer and rising to become senior vice president and chairman of the board of IBM World Trade Corporation.

Armstrong had a B.S. in business and economics from Miami University of Ohio and was a graduate of the advanced management curriculum at Dartmouth Institute. Pepperdine University had just awarded him an honorary Doctor of Laws degree. He was chairman of the President's Export Council, the FCC Network Reliability Council on Foreign Relations, the National Security Telecommunications Advisory Committee, and the Defense Policy Advisory Committee on Trade.

In November 1997, he became the new chairman and CEO of AT&T.

Rick was pleased and relieved—until a conversation with Sunbeam's Al Dunlap shook him up.

The story, as told by AT&T Solutions' COO Brian Maloney, goes like this:

One Saturday afternoon, Rick had to give a talk at an industry conference. Also slated to speak was Al Dunlap of Sunbeam— "Chainsaw Al"—whose definition of executive shuffling was firing everyone in sight. So Rick went up to Al and introduced himself, and Dunlap said, "Oh, you're the AT&T guy. How long do you think you'll keep your job?" Rick ignored this remark and tried to make small talk, and then he asked Al, "If you were taking over AT&T, what would you do?" And Al said, "I'd start by firing the top deck." And Rick said, "I just got to the top deck." And Dunlap went on, "Fire the top deck, bring in my team, and start over. Then, I'd jack up the board a little bit, too."

Now it was time for Rick to give his speech, but he was distracted. It was one of the few times I'd ever seen him riled. Afterwards he found Dunlap and said, "You wouldn't fire everybody, would you? You'd look around and keep who was good." And Dunlap replied, "I guess I'd probably spend an hour with each of the top managers and try to sift out who was good and bad, but I'd still fire half of them. You gotta create change."

So Rick left, glad that Dunlap wasn't running AT&T. Then first thing Monday morning he told us what Dunlap had said. And then he said, "I've got an hour with the Chairman on Wednesday, one-on-one: I've got to be prepared." And we started in on him,

"Well, it's been nice knowing you, boss, good luck," and stuff like that. And then we helped him put together 200 view graphs— that's the engineer in him—and he got ready to tell the whole story of how AT&T Solutions was doing just great. Then he went in to see Armstrong—

Here Rick picks up the story:

I told Mike that the growth potential in networking was unlimited. I predicted that AT&T would either be a leader in the market or wish it had been. And I said I feared that if he didn't support AT&T Solutions personally, full-scale, and without delay, our golden opportunity would slip away.

Without delay—damn the torpedoes—full speed ahead.

Rick's appeal conveyed a pulsing, surging need for speed—a culture of speed, in fact.

Now the questions were, Would the AT&T corporate culture as defined by its new CEO be nimble, bold, and aggressive enough to support the AT&T Solutions culture in a clinch? Could it align with AT&T Solutions' vision? Would Mike Armstrong see that AT&T Solutions' mission was vital to AT&T's corporate mission as well?

"Mike surprised me," says Rick. "He didn't want to look at wall charts or notes. He just sat back and recalled that IBM had dragged its feet getting into outsourcing while he was at Big Blue, and thus EDS had grabbed an early lead. He didn't want that to happen at AT&T. And then he said to me, 'You're the first person who's come to me today and offered to build a $5 billion business.' He liked that. And he gave us his support on the spot."

AT&T Solutions CTO Dick Anderson believes Armstrong was ready to support AT&T Solutions that morning even before Rick walked in.

"Mike wanted to make AT&T much bigger and much more successful, not just inch along. I think he already recognized that AT&T Solutions—with its small size, its proactive model, and its nimbleness— spurred growth. In fact, Rick inspired all of us to say, 'Let's not grow at 5 percent. Let's grow at 50 percent. Why not! Let's not even consider why not, let's just figure out how to get it done.'

"I believe what Armstrong appreciates most about AT&T Solutions is that we don't acknowledge constraints."

Even though Armstrong hadn't asked Rick to prove AT&T Solutions could reach $5 billion, Rick wondered if he should prove it to himself.

"I may have been a little ambitious," Rick admits. "You get caught up in the vision and the ambition, and then you realize this is a heck of a lot of growth that has to be sustained year after year nonstop. And the creative side of me says, 'This is wild, go for it,' and the engineering side says 'Wait, hold it, figure it out.' Finally you ask yourself, 'Is $5 billion a year an achievable goal?' And you answer, 'Well, I believe it is, and the chairman of a very powerful corporation believes it is, and all my colleagues do, too, and that's good enough for me.'"

What does Armstrong himself have to say on all this?

"Mastering and leading fast-changing technology is one of the major business challenges today," he asserts. "Otherwise, you become a follower and your competitors leave you behind.

"I remember back when I was president of IBM's data processing division for sales and service. This fellow showed up in my territory from EDS named Ross Perot. He kept winning accounts from our control to his control. I might keep some of the business in my mainframes and software maintenance, but he got account control. Then, in early 1983, IBM permitted me to be an independent business unit. They said to me, 'We're going to protect you, and you're going to be an independent business unit in our smokestack culture. We are going to measure you on growth, and you have to go after account control.'

"Then, when I came to AT&T and I first met with Rick, I told him, 'Rick, if there's anything this company must be, it's customer-centric and market-focused. Now, we've got to do for you what IBM did for me. I'm going to protect you, and what you've got to do for this company with all this protection is grow your business like hell.' And that's just what he did."

In this first encounter between the Armstrong-era AT&T culture and the AT&T Solutions culture, the two aligned perspectives and joined forces to affirm

A Culture of Vision
A Culture of Courage
A Culture of Honesty and Integrity

A Culture of Excellence in Business Arts

A Culture of "To Be" (leaving "not to be" out)

A Culture of Speed (not barreling out of control but cruising at a fast-paced clip)

A Culture of Dreams

A Culture of Belief

Mike Armstrong's support of AT&T Solutions was not his only bold, expansionist stroke. In 1998 he embarked on a mission to grow the corporation far beyond its pure long-distance roots and to gather assets that would help make it a global communications company of the first rank. In that year, he spent $45.9 billion in purchasing Teleport Communications Group, Tele-Communications, Inc., and Vanguard Cellular Systems, Inc.

In addition, AT&T launched a global joint venture with British Telecommunications, creating an enterprise called Concert to serve multinational business customers, international carriers, and Internet service providers.

"The AT&T/BT global joint venture is designed to provide better service for its customers and economic growth for its shareholders," said Armstrong. "It reflects our belief in the future of an open, competitive global telecom market. We're not only investing our hopes in that kind of market, we're investing our resources as well."[6]

And Armstrong wasn't through. Additional Internet, wireless, and global enterprises were in his sights, as well as more mutually enriching partnerships with cable companies.

CHAIRMAN ARMSTRONG'S VIEWS: A BIGGER, STRONGER, AND BETTER AT&T

"We can't stand back and let the future unfold. I can't think of a single revolution in history that worked that way."

"As the management theorist Peter Drucker writes, 'In the mental geography of e-commerce, distance has been eliminated. There is only one economy and only one market.' This is the concept that telecom companies have lived with for years—what analysts refer to as 'the death of distance.'"

"We're investing in cable to provide broadband connection to homes and businesses. Those broadband connections will allow us to offer customers five new services: telephony, digital TV, high-speed Internet access, interactive TV, and small business communications."

"Recently, a lot of what we offered was based on a resale strategy. We made contracts, we had alliances, and we did franchising. But basically, we were reselling our competitors' stuff. We've realized this isn't a durable approach. It isn't even in line with human nature. So, to offer the kind of value our customers want, we have to be facilities-based. This means offering a seamless set of services, functions, features, performance, reliability, and cost that extend around the world and support our customers as they take their business to their own customers."

"AT&T is willing to make the investments necessary to compete in the new economy. Our goal is to transform AT&T

- From a company that relies on narrowband to one that makes full use of broadband
- From a company that switches circuits to one that switches packets
- From a domestic company to a global communications business
- From a long-distance company to an 'any distance, any service, any source' company"

Clearly, this was no longer your father's AT&T. This was not the steady-as-she-goes AT&T corporate culture of the past.

This was an AT&T Solutions–style, bull-by-the-horns approach—and in this soaring culture of dreams and belief, AT&T and AT&T Solutions were flying wing-to-wing.

As we will see in Chapter 6, a drive to forge strategic alliances was a shared cultural trait.

DEBRIEFING

Acculturation

In highlighting key elements of corporate culture, we'll stick with the noun-verb approach:

The Noun

That was then (a generic worst-case company):
A culture that was nearsighted, tentative, self-protective, satisfied with the status quo, sometimes unsure of its own reason for existence, slow to respond to challenges and opportunities, hung up on concrete reality, and bent on wishful thinking instead of inspired by wishes themselves.

This is now (a best practices company—yours perhaps?):

A Culture of Vision
A Culture of Courage
A Culture of Honesty and Integrity
A Culture of Excellence in Business Arts
A Culture of "To Be" (leaving "not to be" out)
A Culture of Speed (not barreling hell-for-leather but cruising at a
    fast-paced clip)
A Culture of Dreams, Belief, and Daring-Do

Be honest: Which culture does your company have?

The Verbs

Get with the Program—Today

If your culture is the old, outmoded one, here's what to do: Examine, analyze, deconstruct, redesign, rearrange, and rebuild your old paradigms into a dynamic, fast-paced culture fit for current challenges and opportunities.

In short: Acculturate!

Everyone who has come into AT&T Solutions—from AT&T and from outside—has had to acculturate from traditional ways of doing business to doing it at the speed of change.

Is acculturating easier said than done?

No, it's easier done than merely said, because talk alone gets you nowhere.

Here's more of what to do:

Give Everyone a Running Start

The bad news is that even to become pathetic, most companies' orientation programs would need to be upgraded by a factor of 10. The good news is that some companies like AT&T Solutions already have superb orientation programs, and these are being upgraded to even higher levels every day.

Some suggestions:

1. If you don't currently have an orientation program, start one.
2. If you do have an orientation program, but it lasts less than 2 days, enhance and extend it. (Remember, AT&T Solutions sends all new hires through a 5-day orientation program within their first month on the job.)
3. Make sure your program introduces the culture of the organization in addition to laying out policies and rules.

Reduce Your Policy Manual by 50 Percent

First Union Bank President Ken Thompson stated his company's policies to his employees in this way: "We must rededicate ourselves to solving customer problems. That means we must do what the customer asks us unless it is illegal, immoral, or unethical."

The entire policy manual of Seattle-based Nordstrom reads: "Use good judgment in all situations. There will be no other rules."

Your company can't be leading at the speed of change if it's plowing through reams of policy prose. Less policy—as long as it's good policy—brings more good results. In the new economy, policy wonks finish last.

Here's the policy-shaping plan you should adopt:

1. Cut your policy manual to half its present length.
2. Six months from now, reduce it another 50 percent.

Chapter

6

Building Winning Alliances

"Peace, commerce, and honest friendship with all nations," said Thomas Jefferson, "entangling alliances with none."

Rick Roscitt could have written this himself, particularly the part about alliances.

"Like most big companies, AT&T found alliances threatening and countercultural," says Rick. "Whereas we at AT&T Solutions couldn't have survived without them."

Why were alliances essential to AT&T Solutions' survival?

"The technology was too vast," says Rick, "we couldn't cover it on our own. Alliances enhanced our capabilities and stretched the limits of who we could serve and what we could do."

Though AT&T Solutions started small, it set its sights high and wide.

"Companies that are comfortable being small or pure niche don't need to partner in a big way," explains Rick. "They can just borrow income-statement or balance-sheet items. To be global, though, you have to exchange technology, platforms, and complementary skill sets.

You have to join your names and publicity machines. That way you capture worldwide business segments. You cover much more ground."

An early AT&T Solutions partner was John Chambers, president and CEO of Cisco Systems.

No wonder. Chambers was a dreamer and believer, too.

"John could have done quite well without giving us the time of day," says Rick. "But he decided to personally help me launch AT&T Solutions. He went miles out of his way."

What would Chambers gain by helping AT&T Solutions?

"Good question," says Rick, "since this was before we'd done Merrill Lynch and there was no guarantee of our ultimate success. But John has brilliant business instinct, plus an alliance mentality. He saw that we'd provide Cisco with network solutions and, as we grew, that we'd buy in aggregate for our clients and throw huge amounts of this business Cisco's way. His foresight was perfect, of course."

For AT&T Solutions, Chambers became both a business ally and a vocal booster in the marketplace. "He believed in our vision and where we were going and he wanted others to believe in us, too. I'm forever grateful to him for that."

AN INTERVIEW WITH
JOHN CHAMBERS

Bill Capodagli: Rick Roscitt told us that he appreciates not only the partnership between AT&T Solutions and Cisco, but also the advice you gave him during the start-up of his new company. What advice would you give anyone in establishing an alliance such as the one you have with AT&T Solutions?

John: I'd first start with the assumption that most alliances and strategic partnerships fail. So you have to say, "What are we going to do differently so we don't fail, too?" It won't be a question of I'm going to be smarter or work harder. To succeed, a strategic partnership alliance has to be worth a lot of revenue to both companies, enough to keep the top managements focused and committed to allocating resources. There is no such thing in my opinion as a 50/50 transaction. It's going to be 60/40, 30/70. Partnerships are hard to do unless your top management really believes that the benefit is there and they're totally committed to pursuing it. With AT&T Solutions, this means Rick and Mike Armstrong have to be on board. Unless they really buy into the approach, it won't go. Plus, your company's culture has to accept it. If the culture doesn't believe in partnering and doesn't accept its value—even if top management buys into it 100 percent—it won't go down through the organization. Also, you have to create a sustainable competitive advantage. All of these elements are key.

If you look at companies in the technology and computer markets during the 1980s, they did it largely by themselves. These were the IBMs, the DECs, and the HPs of the world. They were largely a vertical market. During the 1990s, the ones who were successful learned how to acquire. As I said, the majority of acquisitions fail, and I'll use AT&T as an example. They put themselves into a very good position with their acquisition strategy. And we did the same thing with Cisco; we acquired over 61 companies. We had to rewrite the textbooks about acquiring, and acquiring was every bit as difficult as we thought. In my industry, the failure rate was even higher than in service products. Failures probably exceeded 75 percent in acquisitions done. Most people would say Cisco's hit rate was probably in the 85 to 90 percent range, so compared to everyone else we were off the charts in terms of our success.

In the coming decade, the companies who succeed will be those who know how to partner strategically. They'll be the ones who win.

In many ways, Rick was the champion of the Cisco relationship with AT&T. We agreed that this market was changing at an incredible pace—what I call Internet pace. It's interesting to watch this market mutate. From one angle it looks one way, from another angle another way. If you take just one angle you won't get the whole picture. By taking them all you can see how it's evolving overall.

Nothing tightens a relationship like common customers. With AT&T, we started off working the revenue opportunities with Rick—figuring out what worked and what didn't work and how to do what should be done. That kept us focused. We did the same with our acquisition strategies—we learned from the first several, then replicated successful concepts and drove them at a faster pace. That's how you get your revenue.

Lynn Jackson: Could you describe how your partnership has evolved over time and what sustains it?

John: There's a unique thing about Mike Armstrong and Rick Roscitt that attracts me to partnering with them. When there are bumps—which there will be in any situation—they don't say, "Hey, we've got a problem with our partner." They say instead, "Okay, there's a problem, now how do we resolve it together?" One time it may be 75 percent Cisco's issue and 25 percent AT&T's. Another time it's the other way around. So, rather than pointing fingers in the old-style way, we communicate candidly about where we both are.

It's in periods of stress that each company sees what the other is really like. A network problem we had two years ago was a defining moment of our partnership. At that time, the relationship could have gone either way. I called Mike Armstrong from Tokyo in the middle of the night and told him what was wrong. Most partners would say immediately, "It's your fault." But Mike's response was, "All right, we've got a problem. How do we turn it into a winner?" He saw problems as opportunities. And Rick, Frank Ianna, and the rest of the AT&T Solutions group approached this the same way. "Let's fix the transaction. Let's fix the problem," they said, "and let's use this as a chance to get our companies closer together, not further away." Our partnership was even tighter after that.

When Mike decided to acquire the cable companies, we invited him to come out here and spend a day with us. He brought his whole team and we outlined strategy for how we could be a partner in this major new opportunity.

Bill: What challenges will there be in leading in this new economy?

John: The challenges are going to very simple. The fast are going to beat the slow. The key factors will be talent, speed, and branding. Those who evolve too slowly get left behind, and those who don't move will cease to exist. And leaders will have to walk the talk. In other words, you can't say one thing and do another. Last week, as an example, I had 18-hour days, five keynotes a day, four customers at the end of the day, and probably 10 to 20 press articles being generated. But the leader sets the pace for the organization. The team can't go faster than the lead dog. If you're serious about revenue growth, if you're serious about the competition, the leader has to walk the talk. Both Mike and Rick do that very well.

Though Cisco Systems had emerged as an independent enterprise while AT&T Solutions was born of Mother AT&T, both John Chambers and Rick Roscitt were classic entrepreneurs.

"Entrepreneurs almost always form alliances," says Rick. "They know that independence comes through strength, and that strength is in numbers. Alliances are magic—they make you bigger and more powerful than you are."

Magic might well describe certain "virtual corporations" that produce nothing more tangible than alliances and yet market real products under their own brand names.

"Nike really doesn't make sneakers," says Rick. "They don't even own the factories or the raw materials. They don't even sell the shoes themselves. They just transfer them to retailers who do. So there are no direct Nike customers per se."

Which means there's a "swoosh" logo but no real Nike sneaker.

"Nike designs the product and promotes it with star talent," says Rick, "but the company itself has no talent whatsoever for actually making shoes."

Another example is Dell, which assembles, configures, brands, and ships other manufacturers' components but manufactures no computer parts of its own.

Is AT&T Solutions a virtual corporation?

"If virtual means extending your power and reach through alliances," says Rick, "then we are."

How does AT&T Solutions choose its alliance partners when, as John Chambers said, most partnerships fail?

"It's like a marriage with a prenuptial agreement," says Scott Perry, AT&T Solutions' vice president of business strategy. "You create the divorce before you tie the knot."

But why anticipate divorce?

Explains Rick: "At root, each company is selfishly motivated to take care of its shareholders. As long as the alliance helps them do that, they stay in love. But once it doesn't, and one company gets cold feet, the marriage can blow apart."

Are some alliances doomed from the start?

"Absolutely," says Scott, "the ones that are concocted just for publicity. The ones that aren't designed to serve customers and aren't prepared to weather the storms and absorb the bumps in the road. The ones where each company ends up competing directly or through other partners. The ones where one sales force calls the other sales force dumb."

Adds Rick, "Alignment of the companies' cultures is critical. They both must be win-win. If one company is just out to take care of itself, the alliance won't work."

A partnership's mere duration, Rick suggests, is not the final test of its strength. "If both companies grow their enterprises and serve their clients better during the collaboration, no matter how long it lasts, then the alliance is a success."

Said otherwise:

If I'm okay, you're okay.

If I fail, you're down the tubes, too.

Failure often comes from one side pulling the other too hard. When this happens, it's best to meet in the middle.

"A strategic partnership involves strategic compromise," Rick says. "We say we'll yield on this point if you give some strategic ground. But there has to be mutual trust. If you're not sure about your partner's honesty, then do a couple of trial tactical deals. If you're satisfied after that, tie the knot."

Compromise is not achieved with a magic wand, of course. It takes work—especially when R&D shops are involved.

"Both companies have these development labs," Scott notes, "and guess what, they're both working on the same issues. So we do a series of continuing and lengthy dialogues about which lab should sacrifice what. Sometimes the labs don't give an inch, and when they don't, the senior leaders have to literally tell them, 'We're killing your favorite project in favor of our strategic partner's project. Sorry, but that's that.'"

Such conflicts are worst between two large corporations.

"Big companies find it hard to compromise," says Rick. "They get so stuck in their ways. At the start they say, 'Yes, we want a win-win relationship,' and then they just go for the win."

These inflexible partners must realize that collaboration demands compromise and a free sharing of assets and attributes.

"It's a real challenge for us to find compatible partners," Scott says, "especially large ones with broad agendas, complex financial and research machinery, and entrenched product lines."

In the year following Rick's appointment as AT&T Solutions' CEO and Armstrong's as head of AT&T, the following story broke:

THE WALL STREET JOURNAL
WEDNESDAY, DECEMBER 9, 1998

AT&T TO PAY $5 BILLION FOR IBM NETWORK
Deal Jump-Starts Effort to Build Infrastructure for Global Data Traffic

In the early 1980s IBM had established its Global Network to sustain most of its internal communications and to support the delivery of its services to its customers worldwide. By 1998 though, the costs of staying technologically competitive—hundreds of millions of dollars a year—had become too great.

Simultaneously, Rick and Armstrong were agreeing that AT&T's own investment in information infrastructure did not serve its core businesses—especially in the new networking age.

In the new arrangement, about 5000 IBM network employees became AT&T employees, and more than 2000 AT&T applications processing employees went to IBM.

In addition, AT&T Solutions took over as a supplier for many of the 1000 telecommunications companies that had been working on the network for IBM.[1]

"Our two companies found each other and made a swap," says Bill Etherington, currently senior vice president and group executive for sales and distribution at IBM.

BILL ETHERINGTON'S STORY: A PARTNER'S VIEW

Essentially, we traded our digital IBM Global Network over to AT&T, and they handed us the operations of a lot of their computing infrastructure. It was a natural alignment, and it gave each company an even stronger platform on which to work. And it served both of our customers better, too.

I've been in this business 37 years, and for the first 35 years there was only one way to justify an investment: to save money. In the last two years almost everything we do is justified not by saving money but by enhancing our competitive product offerings and reaching new markets.

Today each machine has everybody else's chips in it. But how do the machines interconnect? No one can provide a complete end-to-end solution for that. So we form partnerships. A good partner is one who complements what you have in a total solutions sense—hardware, software, and services—so in that regard you're responding to your market. But you're also responding to your partner's culture. You have to be able to align with it. There have to be cultural links.

It's hard for us to partner with a very small company. It is much easier for us to partner with an AT&T because our cultural heritage is the same. We're both large organizations, we're both global, and we're managed by professional leaders who can trust each other and agree on mutual objectives and see the market from a common point of view.

Mike Armstrong came from IBM, and he was my boss at one time. Lou Gerstner has been on the board of AT&T. So there's a rapport that goes way back.

The AT&T Solutions culture is very customer driven. Ours is too. We both see companies not wanting to buy all the pieces and assemble them themselves, so we join forces to solve their networking problems in a bigger, more comprehensive way.

Rick is comfortable in an alliance. He's a straight-shooter at the conference table, very positive, never protesting that he can't do something for the customer, but always saying, "Yes, we'll find a way."

Alliances are complex. They're really a four-way street. We're AT&T's largest client in the world, for example, while they're a huge one of ours, too. At the same time, we go to market together selling solutions to our partnership's customers. In the last sense, as separate companies, we're competitors for some of the same accounts. If our two cultures weren't aligned and locked into each other, those four crosswinds would tear our alliance apart.

"What's really unfolding is a partnership between IBM and AT&T," affirmed Berge Ayvazian, executive vice president of Yankee Group.

It was ironic that IBM—which once upon a time hadn't believed that it was time to get into networking or that it should be AT&T Solutions' partner in ventures of this sort—ultimately lost both disbeliefs.

A key participant in the new arrangement, AT&T Solutions could take hearty pleasure in bonding with a company that three years earlier had blown them off.

AT&T Solutions' view of the partnership is provided by a stalwart player we know well by now—Gerry Pape.

GERRY PAPE'S STORY, PART 3: IBM

I took over the IBM deal in 1999. It is the largest contract for AT&T Solutions to date—more than a billion dollars per year. We operate this engagement on a different model than the typical outsourcing contracts. This deal originated with AT&T's purchase of IBM's Global Network and included the outsourcing contract that I manage serving IBM and a large base of their customers.

What is unique about this deal, in addition to its size, is that we have an outsourcing contract with IBM, who themselves are an outsourcer. An outsourcer of an outsourcer has its unique challenges and opportunities. We provide a value proposition that IBM ultimately passes on to the technology's end users. Value is created by the end users achieving their goals, not by me and my IBM counterparts meeting every day.

Customers want delivery yesterday, and value is created by giving them that. We have to build the technology, the process, and the architecture, plus send the right people out to do the work. We've got to do this faster than ever before. IBM expects it. The end users demand it. And we demand it of ourselves. We're beyond where we were with Chase and Merrill Lynch. The need for speed is even more intense.

Scott Perry has noted the difficulty in partnering with companies that have broad agendas, complex financial and research machinery, and entrenched product lines.

Since IBM was as large, complex, and entrenched as they come, it was inevitable that AT&T's acquisition of IBM's Global Network would bond the two companies but also set off some sparks.

SCOTT PERRY'S STORY, PART 1:
PARTNERING WITH IBM

Our alliance with IBM was founded on our mutual outsourcing deals and our go-to-market partnership. We then sought to extend the alliance into e-business solutions, but it was easier said than done. We thought of e-business as a networking phenomenon, and they thought of e-business as a perfect opportunity to sell more services, software, and hardware. We could rationalize the difference into a cooperative agenda, but then we got stuck at the customer interface. Who owned the customer at that point?

To avoid outright conflicts of approach, the question became, Which projects should be supported and which should be dropped? And both companies' sales departments confronted turf issues of similar sorts.

Remember that AT&T and IBM came into partnership from distinct arenas of success. They looked at us as a telco, and we saw them as a computer company, and neither of us thought the other could understand e-business as a result. There was an intrinsic lack of trust.

I think the firms that are successful in this increasingly collaborative IT industry are those that figure out how to compete on one day and cooperate on the next.

Still, almost all big partners with broad agendas will remain your competitors in some respects. Just bite your tongue when a partner makes an announcement that is counter to your interests. Because they're often talking about another segment of their strategy, not the one that involves your partnership. You just have to say, "This is a gray world, and that's a black announcement. We'll make a white announcement with them in two weeks."

In some senses, our IBM relationship was like that. There were arenas where we competed very directly for services, businesses, e-business, and big outsourcing contracts. But we also found ways to collaborate. The lesson is, if you decide on the one hand where you want to be good, and on the other where you won't spend your time, you can reduce areas of competition.

Partnering is a matter of creating upsides for both firms. Success today depends on strength in capital, skills, or market position. Or some of the above or all three. No one has enough resources. The industries are skill-short. No one has enough capital to build and support global businesses. So you find elements of your strategy and resources that you can link with the other firm's. If dialogue occurs at a high enough level, these alliances can be built.

IBM's Bill Etherington says this about partnering with AT&T Solutions: "We were both in the solutions business now, so we got into some debates. For example, regarding hosting customer systems: What was networking hosting and what was IT hosting? What was the real difference, and who should be doing which? It got messy because there's a very blurry line between the two."

Would the AT&T Solutions–IBM partnership eventually find smooth sailing or was it a corporate marriage headed for the rocks?

It could have foundered, in fact, if the respective leaders hadn't been such courageous captains of their corporate souls and masters of their bundled business fates.

Together, they pulled their ships off a potential collision course and anchored them—through a series of strategic compromises—in one particularly rich and welcoming deepwater port:

FOR RELEASE WEDNESDAY, SEPTEMBER 30, 1998

BANC ONE FORMS "TECHNOLOGY ONE ALLIANCE" WITH AT&T, IBM

BANC ONE CORPORATION today announced it has formed the "Technology One Alliance" with AT&T Solutions and IBM Global Services to provide the bank with premier networking and computing services as it creates one of the nation's most powerful franchises in banking and financial services.

With total managed assets of $159 billion and total assets of $124 billion, and with 1500 banking centers in 12 states, Banc One (now known as Bank One as a result of their merger with First Chicago NBD) was the eighth-largest bank-holding company in the United States in 1998.

After bulking up through a series of acquisitions, though, the bank had found that its network infrastructure had grown too large and complex. To retain and strengthen its ability to compete, it needed to bring next-generation electronic banking services to the market right away. To do this, it required outside help.

"Technology was changing so rapidly that we needed to partner with pure players in their space," says Marv Adams, Bank One's CTO.

What did Bank One mean by "pure players"?

"Companies whose core business was networking from bottom to top," Adams explains. "Companies that recruited and developed people for this sole purpose and gave networking all of their engineering and manufacturing support."

What about the expense of hiring outsourcers?

"Our benefits would outweigh the costs. Plus, if we were trying to do this ourselves, it would take longer. There'd be more risk." Under the six-year, $1.4 billion contract, AT&T Solutions assumed management of Bank One's voice, data, and video networks, transforming the company's legacy communications system into a single, proactive, state-of-the-art IP-based platform.

To manage these operations, AT&T Solutions opened a new Global Client Support Center in nearby Dublin, Ohio. The center boasted the AT&T Solutions Global Enterprise Management System (GEMS), the most sophisticated networking platform in the world.[2]

For its part, IBM Global Services signed a seven-year, $420 million contract to manage a majority of Bank One's data center operations, including helpdesk support and mainframe/midrange server management. This entailed expanding the IBM Global Services Delivery Center in Columbus, Ohio, and building a new IBM Technology Center of Excellence in suburban Hilliard, Ohio, to house customer service, operations command and control, technical support, and education and training for employees of IBM and other Alliance members.

AT&T was a big educational contributor, too, granting $50,000 to Ohio State's Fisher College of Business to provide continuing educational services to the Alliance. Also, both AT&T and IBM agreed to work with local academic institutions in developing information and networking technology training.

In addition, the Technology One Alliance members agreed to offer internships and other ongoing training opportunities to graduates of the Ohio State programs.

Like all partnerships—in business and in life—this one needed tuning and adjusting as it went along. Responsible for these tasks were the

Alliance CEOs. On the bank's side these included Executive Vice President Mike Skubik, Executive Vice President Mike Keller, Senior Vice President Jack Compton, and Vice President Mike Kouremetis.

Representing AT&T Solutions was Glenn Swift, the company's general manager for the engagement.

GLENN SWIFT'S STORY

I'm a farm kid. I grew up in Tennessee, and my wife did too. We met in college, married in the '60s. I started work with AT&T when I was 20. I went to night school, undergraduate and graduate, and have worked for AT&T ever since. They gave me new jobs at different locations every 18 months, and then Rick called and said he was starting a new unit and I should come onboard. That meant moving near New York, and I felt at that time that I'd moved enough. So I said, "Thanks, but I'd rather not." He asked how I could be persuaded. I said, "Put me somewhere south of the Mason-Dixon line." He said, "How about Columbus, Ohio?" "That's north of the line!" I said. And then I figured it's close enough, and I said okay.

Before I started work, Rick told me Bank One raised their voices a lot, but they were one of the best partnerships we had. They wanted to focus on their core financial services, and we were their enabler along with IBM. For the bank, the network wasn't an end in itself.

Marv Adams was Bank One's CTO. He wanted AT&T's and IBM's technologies and processes but also the discipline we surrounded them with. Not discipline in the military sense but proactive planning and precise execution, because the bank puts a huge premium on operational excellence. They'll sacrifice speed in the planning and installation phases to make sure it works right the first time.

Bank One grew through a series of mergers and acquisitions over a long period. As a result, their technology was an amalgam of pieces from the banks they absorbed. We went in and designed a new networking architecture and transformed their patchwork into one smoothly functioning system. Now we manage all the zones of their Internet access so that anything going in and out passes through an environment that we control. But we're not just giving them a network in the noun sense. We get upstream into the heart of their business and optimize the network's value. So we're a verb, too, in that sense.

We run our part of the alliance like a business. We have a business manager, a CFO, an architecture, an implementation function, a technology function, and a maintenance function. We have defined processes and logistics, and they produce incredibly consistent results. We're a networking services factory, you could say.

Each partnering company is rewarded according to the success of all three. If IBM's and the bank's financials look good, mine do too. We share financials, in fact. Think of how powerful that is: I know IBM's and Bank One's margins and costs, and they know mine. Instead of hiding information, AT&T and IBM open their books so they can best serve the bank. It's a fascinating collective culture that results from this: everyone pulling together for the common, and thus also the individual, good.

Mike Armstrong puts it this way: he says, "What is our role, just transmitting electrons across a set of wires? No, anyone can do that. Our mission is using our talent, drive, and financial capacity to unleash value." That's what AT&T and AT&T Solutions are really all about.

And here are the words of Glenn's counterpart, speaking from the Bank One perspective:

JOHN SKUBIK'S STORY: A CLIENT-PARTNER'S VIEW

I spent 20 years flying for the Air Force before coming to Bank One. I'm a recovering commercial lender now.

The Technology One Alliance's management board is three senior people from AT&T, three from IBM, and three from Bank One. I'm on it because of my business and technical background. I'm far from being a true technologist, though. I know all the acronyms, but I don't know what they all mean.

The Alliance's projects are really more about business than technology, so the business perspective is essential to making them work. It's a cultural issue, having business drivers and business people responsible for implementing the technology. If technology people propose ideas and the business people don't review them before the technology side delivers the projects, you have problems.

AT&T is very important to the future of our business because less of what we deliver will be in physical form and more will be in digits and bits. Statements will go out over the Internet instead of by bulk mail. Checks and other paper documents will be converted to electronic images and sent that way. To move these things from our banking centers to a central location, we'll use more broadband than trucks. The more we do this, and the more technology evolves, the more we need end-to-end solutions, not just network parts. Our partners have to build and manage the networking technology with our business needs in mind. And that's just what AT&T Solutions does. They arrived in the Technology One Alliance with a good reputation, and their performance has confirmed our trust.

Some partners give you "like for like for less." Rick does this: He takes our specifications, and he tells us what he can do with them, but then he says, "Given the situation and the problem you're trying to solve, have you thought about doing it this other way?" And that opens up whole new possibilities and adds huge value as a result. Because big corporations always have the problem of getting the right resources organized in the best way. In the military we called it getting the tip of the spear to the point of combat at the right moment. AT&T Solutions helps us do that.

Our relationship is evolving. For instance, we were reconnecting our 6000 ATMs to the new AT&T network, but the job wasn't going very well. So I met with Glenn Swift to straighten things out. I said to him, "Bank One knows all about installing ATMs; we installed these machines when they were new. So let us teach you how reconnecting them should be done." He agreed and things went fine after that.

Glenn Swift gives this account of the same episode: "We had a little sharing of emotions over those ATMs. We shared some facts, too. I acknowledged that we could be doing better, and he said fine, let's forget how we got to this point, and let's just keep moving ahead."

The Technology One Alliance was a landmark endeavor in many ways. For example, the AT&T Solutions–IBM alliance was the first-ever integration of multiple IT companies' enterprise management systems to serve a common client. (In addition to partnering with IBM, AT&T Solutions leveraged strategic supplier relationships with Lucent Technologies and Cisco Systems.)

Together, AT&T Solutions' GEMS platform and IBM's Enterprise Systems Management (ESM) solutions gave the Technology One Alliance the most advanced IT management tools available at the time.

By providing common tools and processes, GEMS and ESM enabled all alliance members to integrate their efforts and thus function in step and in synch. From the bank's point of view, GEMS and ESM were a unified whole that was literally greater than the sum of its parts.

Said Bank One's Marv Adams: "The Technology One Alliance helps us by incorporating two high-powered technology and networking companies in our planning process, increasing our competitiveness, and realizing a higher return on our investment in technology."

The contract was AT&T Solutions' largest in its three-and-a-half-year history and the richest networking contract ever in the financial services industry. It brought AT&T Solutions' new long-term business signings in 1998 to $2.5 billion and raised its long-term business backlog to $5 billion.

"We don't want to steal your piece of the pie," Rick had said to IBM in 1995. "We want to work with you to make the pie bigger."

IBM had said, "Who needs you?"

In 1998 Rick proved himself a man of his word.

And IBM proved itself capable of changing its mind when doing so made shareholder sense.

CASE STUDY:
TECHNOLOGY ONE ALLIANCE (TIA)

The following study charts the evolution of the Technology One Alliance from Bank One's point of view. It begins with the initial perception of needs and challenges, tracks the Alliance's achievements to date, and concludes with a view toward future success.

* * * * *

D R E A M

1997: Time for a Change

The Problem

- Customers are being lost because IT services are not meeting the customers' rapidly evolving electronic banking needs.

The Causes

- Bank One has grown into a national financial services company, but its IT function has not built an infrastructure capable of supporting the transformed corporation.
- IT's best people are spending too much time fixing production problems and too little time addressing strategic business issues.
- Emerging Lines of Business (LOBs) have not aligned and integrated their technology teams and plans.
- IT and IT's key partners have lost credibility across Bank One.
- The entire IT function remains in-house despite insufficient skills and failures to meet "process competencies."

The Goal

- To provide consistent, reliable, and profitable electronic banking services to regain lost customers, attract new ones, and optimize value for the bank.

The Strategy

- Transform the people, processes, and technology of IT by
  - Creating and implementing a new IT management structure that promotes greater flexibility, efficiency, stability, and enlightened control.
  - Upgrading IT competency to a level of "best of the best."
  - Properly aligning LOBs and IT.
  - Implementing robust and flexible IT delivery practices to meet strategic business needs.
  - Developing and maintaining key technology skills.
  - Adopting a variable, usage-based cost model.
  - Enabling LOBs to make cost/service trade-offs.
  - Improving overall cost efficiency in the short and long terms.
  - Making the bank's transformation into an e-business priority number one.

DECISION POINT: To Outsource or Not to Outsource?

Options

- Don't outsource at all: keep all IT in-house.
- Keep most IT in-house; outsource narrowly and selectively.
- Build an IT-outsourcing alliance with "Top Gun" pure players.

- Outsource all IT to pure players through an outsourcing "general contractor."
- Outsource all IT directly to a single pure player.

Decision-Making Criteria
- Achieve the best IT, customer service, and overall business results.
- Maintain control over the IT function.
- Maximize speed and efficiency.
- Favor "pure player" services over subcontractor intermediary involvement.
- Be the lead manager in any alliance.
- Minimize hierarchy and bureaucracy.
- Guarantee all players' full accountability.

DECISION: Build an IT-Outsourcing Alliance with "Top Gun" Pure Players

★ ★ ★ ★ ★

B E L I E V E

1998–1999: *The Technology One Alliance— a Virtual Company Is Born*

The Alliance Partners
- Bank One
- AT&T Solutions
- IBM

Value of Services under Contract
- $2.5 billion

Scope of Managed Resources
- 5800 mainframe MIPS
- 25 terabytes of DASD
- 65,000 servers and workstations
- 59,000 e-mail users

- 145,000 voice ports
- 89,000 voice mailboxes
- 4000 data network sites

The Vision: Creating the Virtual Company
Working Relationship

- Establish a governance model that delineates executive authority and functional responsibilities.
- Design a business model that facilitates effective communication, cooperation, and a win-win relationship between partners.
- Assure that all decisions and actions are in the best interests of Bank One employees, shareholders, and customers.
- Align partners' interests and goals.
- Integrate partners' processes and tools.
- Operate with integrity in all aspects of the endeavor.
- Communicate openly and honestly at all times.
- Honor all commitments made to partners and Bank One employees.
- Place overall Alliance success above individual rewards.

Goals and Incentives

- Have the policy board determine Alliance-wide targets based on achievement of shared goals.
- Ensure that partners leverage their performance management and incentive systems to support these shared goals.
- Ensure that partners measure success against shared goals.
- Ensure that all performance rewards are based on achievement of shared goals.

People

- Collaborate with partners to recruit, develop, and retain the best and brightest IT employees.

Operating Principles: Values and Behaviors to Guide Day-to-Day Interactions

- Bank One First—Make the design and timely delivery of the right solutions for Bank One everyone's first priority.

- Delight the Customer—Be responsive and easy to do business with. Do whatever is required to provide quality customer services first and address any contract scope questions later.
- Pure Player Role—Enable the providers to manage and do what they do best as Bank One pure player partners.
- Legitimate Interest—Recognize the interests of all the partners as legitimate and always consider them as decisions are made.
- Personal Accountability—Extend personal accountability for total Alliance success beyond individual roles and responsibilities.
- Earn Trust—Assume individuals are opening with "best intent" and earn trust by communicating openly and honestly and by following through on commitments.
- High Performance—Function as a high-performance, results-oriented team bound together by a shared purpose, aligned goals, and a commitment to continuous learning.
- Great Workplace—Make Alliance a great place to work: value diversity, invest in people, celebrate success, and have fun.
- Think Process—Involve stakeholders, develop the best possible interfaces between steps in processes, clarify process ownership, and use common language.
- Effective Decisions—Always make effective and timely decisions by determining the scope of the issue, involving the right people, and focusing on the facts to determine the best option.

Governance Structure

Policy:
Policy Board

Membership: Senior executives of Bank One, AT&T Solutions, and IBM.

Responsibility: Establish policies.

OFFICE OF CEO

Membership: Alliance partners' full-time leadership.

Responsibility: Interface between the policy board and the executive strategy team.

Strategy:
Executive Strategy Team

Membership: LOB leaders.

Responsibility: Develop strategies to execute policies set by the policy board.

Execution:
Service Teams

Membership:

Production service delivery	Business and partner management
Architecture and technology solutions	LOB relationship management
	Organizational effectiveness
Product delivery	Process integration

Responsibility: Execute strategies developed by the executive strategy team.

* * * * *

D A R E

1999: *First Results: Off to a Flying Start*

Recall Bank One's central problem in 1997:

- Customers are being lost because IT services are not meeting the customers' rapidly evolving electronic banking needs.

The bank's corresponding goal was

- To provide consistent, reliable, and profitable electronic banking services to regain lost customers, attract new ones, and optimize value for the bank.

By the first quarter of 1999, the problem was remedied and the goal achieved. The overall success involved accessory achievements of many sorts:

People
- Assembled, deployed, and maintained "Top Gun" pure player teams.
- Achieved smooth HR transition, raising employee morale and reducing attrition.
- Strengthened leadership and technical skills across the Alliance.
- Upgraded training and development through a mutually reinforcing collaborative approach.

Infrastructure Transformation
- Upgraded and standardized core IT utilities.
- Upgraded and standardized corporate desktops and LAN servers.
- Made significant progress on e-mail transformation.
- Built a dedicated IBM Service Delivery Center and an AT&T Global Client Support Center.
- Consolidated two data centers and integrated them into the IBM Service Delivery Center.

Financials
- Met all financial goals and commitments.
- Met all goals for unit cost improvements, benchmarking, and growth.
- Made significant progress toward basing prices on consumption and service levels.

Corporate Priorities
- Successfully met Y2K commitments.
- Supported all high-priority Bank One initiatives.

- Improved production service delivery processes and performance.
- Supported corporate merger with First Chicago NBD.

NOTE: The day after the Technology One Alliance was formed, Bank One signed a $30 billion merger agreement with First Chicago NBD. Said Mike Keller, Bank One's senior vice president of business and partner management for IT, "The solutions we'll get from AT&T and IBM will help us with the merger." Evidently, they did.

- Brought First Chicago NBD data centers, network, and LAN/desktop groups into the T1A scope.

Alliance Effectiveness

- Developed and refined governance model and overall organizational structure.
- Staffed and strengthened organizational effectiveness team to drive Alliance-wide goal alignment, performance management, communication, and training and development.
- Used case study methodology to turn management system problems into learning opportunities.
- Improved and integrated T1A processes, tools, and culture.
- Cultivated harmonious and productive cross-Alliance teamwork.
- Enhanced and enriched the Columbus, Ohio, community.

★ ★ ★ ★ ★

D o

2000: A New Millennium: Targets for the First 12 Months

NOTE: These goals for 2000 were still being pursued as this book was going to print.

LOB Customer Satisfaction
Availability/Reliability

- Reduce end-to-end repair time to under 2.5 hours in 90 percent of cases.
- Reduce outage minutes by 20 percent for all LOB operations centers.

Delivery
- Complete 97 percent of projects on time.
- Improve cost, scheduling, and quality respectively by 20 percent.

Cost/Capacity
- Meet transformation commitments by fully migrating to target technology.
- Benchmark to achieve "best-in-class" unit cost.

T1A Team Performance
- Continue to attract, develop, and retain the best and brightest employees.
- Sustain and enhance working relationships between all partners' teams.

T1A Financial Performance
- Meet the aligned revenue and expense budget objectives of all partners.

EPILOGUE

Bank One now knows from profitable experience that an alliance blends the skills, ideas, and personalities of people, not just technology's nuts and bolts. Good partners must be firm in asserting their own business interests, as well as sensitive to the professional and personal needs of the whole group.

In this regard, here are some wrap-up thoughts:

- Begin with the end in mind so you know where you're headed from the start.
- Firmly position your company, its employees, and your partners in positions of win-win-win.
- Balance speed with rigor.
- Ensure that LOBs fully participate in the alliance and stay focused on agreed-upon goals.
- Stay attuned to your customers' needs by checking in with them periodically as work proceeds.

- Pursue end-to-end solutions without splitting legal hairs over who's responsible for what.
- Transform your operations at dotcom speed, but be aware that a cultural revolution doesn't happen overnight.

"Forming and sustaining alliances with big companies is not so much a science as an art," reflects AT&T Solutions' Scott Perry. "We're learning the art, though ours is not yet hanging in museums."

Scott's modesty is perhaps unnecessary, given the AT&T Solutions–IBM–Bank One success.

Scott goes on, "We're also learning to work better with the smaller companies where so much of the innovation in software and business models is coming from."

What's the main challenge in partnering with small companies, especially the start-up dotcoms?

Both Rick Roscitt and Scott Perry answer in one word: "Speed."

A case in point is AT&T Solutions' alliance with Seattle-based Data Channel, a leader in the extended markup language field.

Data Channel had been touted by one of AT&T Solutions' outsourcing clients as a master in legacy integration. Scott Perry met with the CEO and worked out a deal whereby

- AT&T agreed to use Data Channel technology and support personnel in legacy infrastructure solutions.
- AT&T invested money in Data Channel at a pre-IPO level.
- Both companies committed to a business and technical dialogue on product development and rollout.
- Data Channel was included in AT&T Solutions' networking management work for corporate AT&T.

From start to finish, the deal took only 45 days to complete.

Only 45 days?

Scott Perry admits that Data Channel achieved a similar agreement with Cisco Systems in less than a week.

"Hey, 45 days was a record for us," says Scott. "And considering the deal had to go through corporate AT&T—the finance people, the CFO, the mergers and acquisitions team, the legal team, and the service line teams—we were pretty pleased."

But they were not totally content. In the future, AT&T Solutions aims to make alliances at Cisco speed. To do this, corporate AT&T and AT&T Solutions will have to align even more closely in streamlining the alliance-forging process and making it central to achieving business growth.

"We have no choice," says Scott. "The small, nimble companies won't wait. They're burning up money with every minute of delay. They've got to create new revenues right now to make up for the cash that's going up in smoke. If we can't help them, they'll look for someone else."

Scott speaks from sad experience: AT&T and AT&T Solutions have bungled some alliances by dragging their feet.

"But we learn from our mistakes," he insists. "As John Chambers says, 'I don't want to do five perfect deals, I want to do ten knowing that eight will succeed and two will fail. Because I learn more from failure than success.' Thanks to Mike Armstrong and Rick Roscitt, we're adopting that same attitude here at AT&T Solutions and AT&T."

Increasing success at the cost of occasional failure—clearly, that's not a bad price to pay. The very fact that AT&T Solutions did not merely tolerate but embraced such a "Fail Forward Fast" bargain signified its arrival on networking's center stage.

Now, having dreamed and believed its way to featured-player status, AT&T Solutions could dare to become a true star.

But first . . .

DEBRIEFING

Alliances

The Noun

To compete in the new economy you must establish alliances with a wide variety of partners, big and small, local and global. They may be feared predators—they may be your former prey.

As John Chambers declared in the foreword to this book, "This decade, leading companies will be those that develop internally, acquire effectively, and form ecosystem partnerships in a horizontal business model. Unlike a vertical business model, in which a single company attempts to excel in every aspect of the business, the horizontal model allows multiple companies to combine their expertise to create comprehensive solutions for their customers."

As we've heard before, "The paradox of the new economy will be that the more power you give away, the more powerful you will become."

The Verbs

Invest in Brainware; Outsource Non-Essentials

Bank One's IT people were fixing network problems instead of using IT to exploit the company's core business opportunities.

The Technology One Alliance turned that the other way around.

What does your company make that outside specialists could make better and cheaper instead?

Customize Your Strategic Alliances

AT&T Solutions deals one way with Cisco and another way with IBM.

All alliances should create efficiencies and economies, but all shouldn't be identical in shape, size, and detail.

Synergy admits of variety.

Symbiosis takes many forms.

Is your company strategically allied?

Are you and your partners all aligned in the exact same way?

Make sure each of your working relationships is designed to address its own issues, goals, and concerns.

Great alliances require trust, communication, and management alignment that create mutual codependencies.

The phrase "one size fits all" does not apply where strategic alliances are concerned.

Don't Play the Blame Game with Partners

When Cisco's John Chambers had a problem with AT&T Solutions, he called Mike Armstrong from Tokyo in the middle of the night. Instead of immediately blaming Cisco or assuming the problem was AT&T Solutions' fault, Armstrong acknowledged the trouble and pledged to collaborate with Cisco in working it out.

This was typical of how all AT&T Solutions leaders dealt with Chambers. In times of stress, they didn't fall back on the contract to defend their actions. They didn't split legal hairs.

"They saw problems as opportunities," Chambers relates. They said, "Let's use this as a chance to get our companies closer together, not farther apart."

Ask yourself the following questions to determine whether you are ready, willing, and able to forge partnerships.

"Yes" answers are green lights. "No" responses are yellow or red.

Is your technology too vast for you to cover on your own? (Does it stretch the limits of whom you can serve and what you can do?)

Is your enterprise global, or does it aspire to be? (As opposed to being small and pure niche?)

Is your top management totally committed to partnering?

Does your corporate culture accept and embrace the value of partnering?

Does your corporate culture align with your partner's culture?

Are you prepared to cooperatively solve problems with your partner rather than laying blame?

Will partnering result in better service to your customers rather than just a splash in the press?

Can you avoid competing directly for accounts with your partner?

If you compete with your partner for some accounts, are your cultures sufficiently aligned to withstand the competitive stress? (Are you prepared to compete one day and cooperate the next?)

Will your partnership be win-win for both parties? (As opposed to your seeking a sole win for yourself?)

Can you trust your partner to deal with you honestly? Can your partner trust you?

Will you and your partner share assets and attributes to avoid duplicating each other's work?

If you and your partner are working on similar projects, can you avoid turf disputes by agreeing upon which projects should be supported and which should be dropped?

Does your company justify its investments in terms of enhancing your competitive product offerings and reaching new markets? (As opposed to just saving money?)

Do you see partnering as a way for companies to complement each
other in a total solutions sense? (Are end-to-end solutions what
you seek?)

Given the size and reach of your company, are you comfortable with
your partner's size and reach as well?

Do your and your partner's leaders see objectives from a common
point of view?

Do your and your partner's leaders have a personal rapport?

Will your partnership increase your efficiency and thus accelerate
your pace of doing business? (Instead of raising complexity and
bogging you down?)

Can you partner with a company that has a broad agenda, complex
financial research machinery, and entrenched product lines?

Are you willing to share financials with your partner?

In assessing the value of partnering, have you fully analyzed your
problem and its causes? Have you laid out your goals and strategies for achieving success? Have you articulated your operational
principles? Do you have a governance structure in mind?

Can you balance asserting your own business interests with simultaneously cultivating value for your partner?

Can you negotiate and close the deal on a partnership with a minimum of red tape and delay?

PART
III

Dare

Chapter

7

Developing Winning Teams

Remember Rick saying that speed is cultural? And that when businesses can't run any faster, they've got to run smarter?

People might mimic this admonition, but many just don't get it. The AT&T Solutions team figured out that the way to run smarter was to clear the road of predictable obstacles, to fail forward fast, and to pick themselves up again. What's really risky is churning along blindly and breaking down or halting in midcourse because we've lost our direction, or run out of steam.

In the culture of dreams and belief we need to be swift of foot—but we've got to dare to run smart.

"There's a skill shortage in our industry," says Rick, "and before it gets better it'll get worse."

For a company bent on 50 percent growth, a skill shortage is cause for grave concern.

"Hunger for knowledge and an unquenchable thirst for higher skills must be prime cultural traits," Rick continues.[1]

Who can satisfy this hunger and slake this thirst? How will skills and awareness be imparted efficiently, effectively, and quickly enough to cultivate the brains—as well as the brawn—to win in today's race?

"I have a great deal of respect for academia," says Rick. "When they get it right, they get it very right. But they're not always on the front lines of what's happening in the world, and I think they missed this networking trend."[2]

It's not just the unenlightened course curricula that Rick laments; it's the whole plodding academic approach.

"We've got to wake up all these professors wandering around brick-and-mortar campuses, teaching only what's in books."

What's wrong with books?

"They only contain what's already happened, not what's at the leading edge. By definition they're out of date!"

So what's needed is real-time learning, right?

"Education and training have to live and breathe and move at the speed of light. They can't do that in the classic classroom because a classroom is a static place. It's a noun in a sentence without a verb, a subject without an action. That old model doesn't cut it today, so we're blowing it up."

Rick's aim is not to raze the bricks and mortar, create a huge rubble pile, and leave it at that. With funding from the AT&T Foundation, he's helping to build a new, flexible, sleek, and sheer educational edifice in its place—the AT&T Education Alliance.

To start, Rick invited Ohio State, Miami University, North Carolina State, North Carolina A&T, and Stevens Institute of Technology to jointly develop curricula addressing business and technological issues, as well as the social concerns raised by globalization and customers' increasing demands for 24/7 service.

Did he really expect educational institutions, which notoriously fight tooth-and-nail for top students, to join hands and minds in common cause?

But as a confident facilitator, Rick succeeded in making the universities feel safe enough to share ideas and strategies, and learn from each other instead of compete.

This delicately balanced education alliance was modeled on a successful business partnership—AT&T Solutions' Technology One Alliance with IBM and Bank One. Just as an executive committee governed the Technology One Alliance with members from each company, so the Education Alliance is steered by a similarly styled panel representing each university. This panel works closely with the various faculties as well as with the leaders of AT&T. They meet once a year face-to-face, and they meet frequently via video conferencing. Though separated by physical geography, they use their own virtual technology to stay in touch.

ECONOMICS 101
"THE AT&T EDUCATION ALLIANCE"

Guest Lecturers:
Tom Hogan, manager, university relations, AT&T Solutions; executive director, AT&T Educational Alliance

Dr. Dan Short, dean, Richard T. Farmer School of Business, Miami University

Dr. Nino Masnari, dean, College of Engineering, North Carolina State University

Dr. Joseph Alutto, dean, Fisher College of Business, Ohio State University

Dr. Quiester Craig, dean, School of Business and Economics, North Carolina A&T University

LECTURE 1: "Education: Who Needs It?"
Tom Hogan
A workplace study by the Information Technology Association of America shows that half of all newly created jobs in our industry are going unfilled.

The reason? An insufficiently well-trained workforce.

The consequence? Fierce competition for the limited quantity of top talent, and a dangerous overburdening of current employees.

The solution to the human capital gap? A fierce new effort to expand and improve education.

Is this effort a logistical nightmare? An academic can of worms? Is it just a pipe dream, in fact?

To Rick Roscitt, it is a dream—but forget about the pipe.

As AT&T Solutions grew rapidly, Rick saw that we needed to attract and retain more and more of the best available personnel. There had to be a pipeline for that human capital fuel. Since one didn't yet exist, Rick went out and started building one. He refused to be passive in the education process; he wouldn't let academic graduates enter the race without the necessary training and skills.

There's self-interest here: we want to attract the best and the brightest to AT&T—and develop their full potential once they join up.

But we also want to expand the talent pool for the whole industry of which we are a part.

LECTURE 2: "An Idea Whose Time Has Come"
Dr. Dan Short

Mike Armstrong told me one day that he was considering giving a million dollars to Miami University to fund a new technology chair. Before he did, though, he wanted assurance that we'd always be on technology's cutting edge.

How could I assure him of that?

With technology advancing so rapidly, how could any university, or any company, always stay out in front?

And then I thought, why always see innovation in competitive terms? Was winning everything? Was it the only thing? And even if it was, did victory always have to mean putting others to defeat?

And then I realized, why not win as a group, and thereby raise our winning odds, and fatten the winning purse?

Specifically, why not partner with other universities and create a combination on-campus and virtual curriculum that would raise skill levels across the board, and give us all a first-place share of innovation's golden cup?

Great idea, said Mike, and gave us the check.

LECTURE 3: "Finding Common Cause"
Dr. Dan Short

It's in our university cultures to be proud of what we do. We blow our own horns quite a bit because we're in stiff competition with other universities to attract the best students. That's our marketplace, and we're all selling our prize-winning faculties and the high quality of our research.

It gets tense. We all think we're the best. And so whenever we're asked to team up with another university, we're wary of compromising our standards to make the partnership work.

AT&T teamed up five universities in the AT&T Education Alliance. Was it a formula for disaster? It could have been if we'd gone straight to working on the technology curriculum. But we were smart, and we addressed cultural issues first. In this way, we opened lines of communication and established mutual trust. Then the leadership teams from each university shared their pedagogical ideas, and the respective faculties began collaborating on course design and content.

Sure, there's been some hesitation, if not outright resistance at times. But we keep in mind what AT&T needs for success from its corporate perspective, just as they look at what the universities need. And that way we all get what we want.

LECTURE 4: "A Garden of Intellectual Delights"
Tom Hogan
How is the AT&T Education Alliance cultivating tomorrow's leaders in communications technology?

Rick Roscitt launched the "AT&T Leaders in Networking Series" with a talk beamed by satellite and Web-cast to the five universities. Rick described networking and AT&T Solutions' role in it, and listed the skills that graduating students must have in order to hit the ground running in their first jobs.

Students loved the presentation and relished the infusion of real-world insights into their academic curriculum. They only regretted not having more time for Q&A. We're adding more interactive time in future events, which will feature Mike Armstrong and other prominent figures from business, government, and academia. Rick himself will be giving additional lectures in the virtual classroom. We also hope that executives from other companies in our industry, including our own clients, will agree to speak.

Another online offering is a course called "Managing the Digital Enterprise," by Professor Michael Rappa. Already hugely popular at Professor Rappa's home campus of North Carolina State, this course will be available to the students of all five Education Alliance Universities, and to the employees of AT&T too.

Of course, the most precious academic resources are the students themselves—and we are eager that as many of them as possible join AT&T. Toward that end, we recruit in person at the five universities.

We also provide full- and part-time internships every year. These give selected students the chance to work with AT&T executives and other personnel, and we intend to hire the top-achievers from these intern groups.

How does the future of the Education Alliance look?

Bigger and better, it would appear. We've been inundated with requests to include other schools, so we may well extend our reach. There's real excitement out there, even more than we anticipated. Academia and the real world are going to be partners for life.

LECTURE 5: "A Two-Way Street"
Tom Hogan

Partners for life.

To promote synergy between the real world and academia, we arrange for AT&T executives to serve on various university advisory committees. Here, they help attune academic curricula to industry conditions today. Some of our people also assume classroom duties as visiting professors and conduct on-campus research.

Simultaneously, we encourage the universities' professors and students to spend time at AT&T to experience firsthand our market challenges. This direct encounter with the real world informs and enriches what they teach.

The AT&T Education Alliance is a mutually enriching crisscross flow of information and insights, not just a one-way street.

LECTURE 6: "New Dogs, New Tricks"
Dr. Dan Short

We're riding a huge, fast-breaking wave of new technology. Older people are adapting to it with various degrees of ease and success. The young people, though—today's students—are taking it right in stride. They're not fighting it, and they're not comparing it to older technology, because this new technology is the only technology they know.

It's like middle-aged people learning French, putting their new French words into English then translating them back into French before they speak a word. Whereas those who learn French as a first language, or as a second language when they are very young, just take it in without great effort. They immediately start thinking and talking and even dreaming in French. They're fluent before they know it.

It's the same with kids today learning the new technology, in high school and in the universities of our Education Alliance. They live and breathe it every day. They see its logic intuitively. It becomes reflexive. Meanwhile, a lot of older people are still struggling to come to grips with it and make it work.

LECTURE 7: "Going the Distance"
Dr. Nino Masnari

Today you can go off to college, or you can get a degree through your computer at home. The death of distance has spawned distance learning, and we're intensively involved in that.

We're giving students access to courses over the Web, so they can study in the evening while working at paying daytime jobs.

Of the 380 master's degrees we delivered last year, 45 went to distance learners, and that number will increase.

I don't say that distance learning will ever, or should ever, replace the on-campus experience for everyone. Campus life helps mature young students both as people and as potential employees. However, for those with financial responsibilities that preclude spending years away from home, our distance learning options are a boon.

LECTURE 8: "Who Wants to Be a Multibillionaire?"
Dr. Nino Masnari

Graduating students in American technology programs are asking themselves today, "Should I go and work for one of these new dotcoms and make a million dollars (or more) before I'm 30? Or should I join and work my way up through a big corporation like AT&T?"

Who can blame the grads who choose the dotcoms? Isn't becoming an early millionaire a common ambition? Isn't their entrepreneurial drive a healthy urge?

In the old days—which weren't so long ago—students saw employment with the big, well-respected companies as a good job for life. Today the dotcom route beckons with its lure of fabulous wealth. "If I'm not rich by 30," says the dotcom new hire, "I'll join a mainstream company after that."

The mainstream companies' challenge thus becomes how to make them join today.

The AT&T Education Alliance is our response to this challenge, and we're seeing some very positive results.

LECTURE 9: "Teen Idols"
Dr. Nino Masnari

Many young people today are forgoing college because they can't resist the huge salaries that companies are offering them. It's a historical first that so many high school kids are commanding such high salaries without a college degree.

The more this trend continues, the smaller our pool of top student candidates becomes. As an academician, I'm naturally concerned about this.

I think it's a mistake for students not to attend college, which seasons them emotionally and socially, in addition to developing their intellectual and technological skills. I understand the financial temptations these people face, but we must convince them that college enormously increases their chances of overall long-term success.

We invite these young people to attend one of our AT&T Education Alliance universities—and get their careers off to the right start.

LECTURE 10: "The Human Touch"
Dr. Joseph Alutto

Today's commercial focus is on the hot new technology, and academia is keen on that, too. But universities are especially concerned about the human aspect of the new economy.

The prime "people" issues, as I see them, are these:

How do you motivate and manage people who view their employment with you as a skill-building phase toward a better job elsewhere, rather than as a job for life in itself?

How do you support people for whom rapid changes in work responsibilities also mean changes in their value to the company?

How do you motivate and manage contract workers?

How do you enable employees to take creative advantage of new technology, and not simply follow orders from above?

Business leads the way in technology today, of course. But we academics have a special responsibility to address technology's human challenges—one of which is enabling five top universities to be productive partners in a bold educational venture, instead of rivals in the research and student recruiting games. In addition, academics must learn to work productively and profitably with the commercial side.

In our Education Alliance, the important human challenges are being met. Under AT&T's enlightened guidance, all Alliance members—commercial and academic—are recognizing and utilizing each other's special knowledge and strengths.

LECTURE 11: "Be All That You Can Be"
Dr. Quiester Craig

Today's fast-changing e-business technology is creating a diversity of new commercial opportunities around the world. We're concerned about e-business workforce diversity here at home.

A lot of bright young students, especially from less advantaged backgrounds, are tempted to make quick fortunes working for dot-coms. A lot of faculty members are tempted, too!

While today's high school students are far more computer-literate than they were just five or six years ago, many of those from lower-income backgrounds are not well versed in business principles. Our university therefore provides practical business experience in addition to classroom training—for those students who arrive highly skilled and knowledgeable, as well as for those who need a leg up.

I know that some community college students are being pushed to accept well-paying jobs after graduating instead of pursuing four-year college degrees. I'm concerned about that. By hurrying into the job market without the deeper skills and knowledge that universities can provide, these young people are headed for a glass ceiling, I'm afraid. Instead, they should get the most education they can, and then become the leaders of the next several decades, not just the hot recruits of tomorrow or the day after that.

Even some students at our own institution are split between studying and earning a check. Many are working at well-paid part-time jobs while they're enrolled as undergraduates. As a result they take six and seven years to graduate, instead of four. Some begin working full-time and don't graduate at all. We must work hard to retain these students and make their undergraduate years as enriching intellectually—and ultimately financially—as they can be. Being part of the AT&T Education Alliance gives us a huge advantage in doing that.

"Savvy, well-prepared human capital is very scarce," notes Rick. "There's a skill vacuum in the networking space, so when we see the kind of person we need—from our own programs or from other institutions—we make an offer on the spot."

Alas, the offers are not always accepted as so many engineering and MBA grads today are heading straight to start-up IPOs. (A job on Wall Street is passé.)

"Recruiting is crucial at AT&T Solutions and it's everybody's job to do it," states Rick. "We're all looking out for people we'd like to work with. We always need new blood."

What is AT&T Solutions' appeal to recently graduated students? Bill Blinn, vice president of human resources, says "our proven success as a pioneering entrepreneur, our future-focused vision, our e-commerce centered value proposition, and our infrastructure that support everything we do."

New hires at AT&T Solutions quickly and thoroughly learn the ropes. An initial five-day orientation session teaches them first the location of the rest room and the supply closet, followed by the structure of the organization and the functions of its various teams.

Next, AT&T Solutions' leadership presents the company's history, vision, and values, and describes its service lines. Thus begins the new hires' true acculturation, as they share the AT&T Solutions dream and feel the first prideful shimmers of collective belief.

Once on the job, new hires are not pigeonholed and stuck into separate cubicles; they are integrated into broadly functioning operational teams. Over time they are given multiple assignments in diverse functional areas to extend and deepen their skills. By rotating in and out of sales, technical, and operational roles, these employees are groomed—and are encouraged to groom themselves—for long and productive careers as individuals and as members of teams.

The development process is thorough but fast.

Says Managing Partner Patrick O'Malley, "There are so many pieces and, today especially, so little time. Just to talk comfortably with a client, our new people have to learn a great amount very quickly. Then to prepare a really persuasive argument, they have to be much more disciplined, efficient, and self-reliant than they ever were before in their supervised academic classrooms. Now they need to do a lot of reading and studying on their own. They have to become self-educating entrepreneurs."

The fact is, AT&T Solutions is rare in sending personnel from all levels—including new hires—into critical client interactions, so these people must be ready to answer the call.

"Before sending them out, we train them for six months," says O'Malley. "In most companies, employees train five to seven years for that first interface."

Greg Walters, director of organizational and professional development, adds, "We're a culture of speed, which means daily change. Some new employees think our speed was just for start-up, but it's ongoing. To everyone I hire I say, 'Whatever you're doing now, it'll be different in three months. Whatever you're thinking now, you won't be thinking then; you'll be thinking something new.'"

To speed professional development, the recently opened AT&T Solutions Learning Lab in Florham Park provides continuous, self-guiding, PC-based training at a sprint-like pace.

Self-starting, self-motivating training does not exclude developmental feedback at critical points.

"We give new hires a mentor, a coach," explains COO Brian Maloney. "AT&T Solutions doesn't sell products. We're a professional services firm offering talent and skill, so coaching is an absolutely critical job."

Adds Bill Blinn, "We're always debating how formal or informal mentoring should be. Our prime concern is that development programs should be customized for each individual."

The AT&T Solutions Professional Profiling System helps new employees find their way through this fun house of change. The system lets employees record their current baseline skill set online, and then build gap analyses and customized personal development plans.

"In the beginning of the year, you key in your two or three main development needs and how you're going to improve," Walters explains. "At the same time, your coaches submit their own views on your development. When you meet your coaches, you compare assessments and work out a final plan for improvement."

The plan might include more training courses—or it might not. To sharpen financial savvy, for example, an employee might be assigned to shadow someone in the finance department. "The best classroom," says Walters, "is the real world."

A cut above the rest, AT&T Solutions has a holistic view of developing their people. It's real-world, real-time education and training. It draws the quintessence from each individual and builds quintessential teams.

The educational focus isn't just on employees as individuals, of course. In client engagements, individuals are members of tightly coordinated teams, and must be trained as such. This applies not only to AT&T Solutions' own employees, but also to those transferred over by the client according to the terms of the deal.

Teamwork is at the very heart of the organization, which means it's not just team members working together smoothly, but also teams with other teams.

There, of course, have been intramural skirmishes break out between accounting and sales and product management departments—inside and outside of AT&T.

But there have mainly been differences of opinion that are good and usually move the ball forward. The key is a common dedication to a common goal.

LYNN BROWN'S STORY: HUMAN RESOURCES AT THE CUTTING EDGE

I started my career when I was very young at Bell Laboratories. I stayed in the Bell system for nearly 10 years until the divestiture, and then I decided it was time to see the world.

My résumé became pretty diverse. Over 12 years, I participated in start-ups and takedowns. I helped build and rebuild enterprises. I saw the world, all right.

One day I got a call from a senior HR person at AT&T. He said AT&T Solutions was looking for people who weren't in the corporate cookie cutter mold. People like me. He asked if I'd consider heading

up HR for AT&T Solutions' outsourcing practice. I was intrigued.
And so, four years ago, I came back to AT&T.

In HR, we sit in on every single engagement. We're responsible for
determining and shaping all the people elements. We position and transition our own employees into the client's business; we integrate those
the client sends to us; and we help them be productive as they can be.

To do all this, we look at what operating principles will be in effect,
what the sales strategy is, and what margins we're going for. We learn
the client's motivations for outsourcing. We find out if they want to
deal with these people issues now or after the nuts and bolts of the deal
are worked out.

The process is schizophrenic in a way: save money, care for people,
save money, care for people, back and forth. You work with the client
to find a balance.

We give the client's people the same orientation that all our own
new employees get. We teach them AT&T Solutions' history, values,
value proposition, and generally what our culture is all about.

We know that transitioning from their firm to AT&T Solutions
can be an emotional shock. Giving up their company badge after 20
years can be the hardest thing they've ever done, or ever will do. The
strange thing is that most of them stay at their same old desks. They
just change their affiliation from the home team to the outsourcer. In
some ways, nothing's different, but in other ways, everything's new. It's
a roller-coaster ride, and we're sensitive to that. Reminding them that
they're moving from the back office in their former company to the
front lines in ours, helps ease the shock. They're not making the
chemicals or the energy or the soup anymore—they're raising the
whole firm's value by enhancing its technological base. They get
excited by that.

Sometimes we get low performers, but we don't send them back.
AT&T believes anybody can learn anything if they're trained well
enough. By March of every year, employees must complete a development plan stating what they're doing now, what they need to do better, and how they're going to improve by year's end.

We're big on teamwork. Collective effort and mutual respect are
the keys to our success. I've been in companies where the top managers
had the stars on their doors, and the trappings of power mattered a lot.

Personally, I don't care where my office is or where at the table I sit. That's why I fit in at AT&T Solutions. It's the most democratic place I've ever worked.

Here's the biggest thing we teach all employees: never say "no" to a customer. If a job looks too tough, say instead, "Maybe we can't do it exactly like you want it done, but together we can try alternative solutions to find the one that works best." By taking "no" out of our lexicon, we end up with "yes." That's a lesson from Rick.

Of course, saying "yes" sometimes puts us right at the edge of the margin. So my HR people also have to be business people who don't give up a piece of profit that was meant for the bottom line. We do a good job of that. We're as financially savvy as we are people-smart, and in the HR world that makes us unique.

We work hard at our jobs, maybe too hard because sometimes people burn out. We could streamline some processes, avoid duplication of work, be more efficient, and save time in places. That would help.

And we could steal from each other more.

What do I mean by that?

I mean let's not redo what other people have already done. Let's not rewrite already-written books. Let's not impress each other with how many hours we've worked and how little we've slept. Let's not be ashamed to use another employee's ideas—if they're great ideas, use them yourself! The client won't accuse you of plagiarism. They couldn't care less. So copy shamelessly and leverage what you copy to the hilt. We'll save time that way, and time is money. We'll lower our expenses and keep our margins up.

I'm very proud of our low employee turnover: 98 percent of the client's employees accept our initial offer to work for AT&T Solutions, and after five years we have a 90 percent retention rate. In presentations to prospective clients, that's a big selling point—we call it our Value Added Human Resources Approach.

When the transition period is over, my work in an engagement is done. The first paycheck's accuracy is my last responsibility. It's a big job to see that all the insurance options and deductibles and stock purchase options and 401(k) plans are handled right.

HR was two people when I started. We're 12 today. I've hired half my people from outside, and they've joined AT&T Solutions for the same reasons I did.

Mine is not the traditional HR role. It's externally focused. I'm affecting revenue, I'm building value, and that creates marketing collateral for securing additional engagements down the road.

Education, training, and quintessential teamwork are the foundation blocks upon which dream and belief in productive careers are built.

Beyond this, AT&T Solutions dares—and dares its employees to dare—to exceed their own past and current performance and thus enter the rarefied zone where human potential is not just fulfilled but unleashed.

In this superachieving realm no man or woman is an island—which means each individual person works for the good of his or her team.

Which means there are no individual performance awards.

Which, at first, horrified much of corporate AT&T.

"They called it a communist plan," chuckles Rick. "For them the traditional end-of-year individual performance award system was the good old American way."

Clearly, the individual award system did not express a healthy American competitive spirit, but simply let employees say to each other, "I did better than you."

Whereas they should be saying, as members of teams, we all did better than we all did before. And tomorrow, next week, next quarter, and next year we'll all do even better than that.

Although specific, tangible, spendable rewards are important, Rick wanted his employees to make more and more money—not in spot bonuses but in higher salaries that come with promotions that reward outstanding team-centric performance, not personal star turns.

"You'll get performance feedback on what you did well," he explains, "but not more pay for individual good work per se. You'll advance in your career, though, when your efforts achieve a common success—and you'll earn more money for that."

A daring approach to compensation indeed.

There was fear in the air that a storm of complaints was on the horizon.

The complaints, however, didn't come.

"We exceeded the results of the business plan," Rick proudly notes. "And people got paid more in aggregate than they would have almost anywhere else in AT&T. Who could complain about that?"

The rewards were more than financial; they were cultural, too.

"We all felt we owned the client together," says Patrick O'Malley. "We weren't hung up on egos and personal agendas."

The team shared a feeling that they were all in it together, and that winning a team medal was the most noble goal of all.

Of course, teams don't run willy-nilly through an unmarked course. Just as greyhounds need mechanical rabbits streaking ahead of them down the track, and fast horses need jockeys to race them down the homestretch toward the finish line, so business teams need specific business targets and spurs to reach the targets.

"Our company is highly goal oriented," says Rick. "Actually, we're oriented beyond goals. We want to exceed, not just meet our targets, that's our culture. We dare ourselves to surpass ourselves. And so we do."

Sounds so simple when he says it that way.

But it isn't simple, of course. Unleashing instead of just fulfilling human potential is superhumanly challenging work.

Which means it's right up AT&T Solutions' street.

This is where a unique performance measurement system called the AT&T Solutions Goal Deployment Process comes in.

"Initially, it's written top-down," explains Rick. "We set the targets in revenue production, expense management, service and product delivery, and customer satisfaction, all from our leadership point of view."

At which point the leadership says: Bottoms Up.

"Then we ask our employees for their input. We give them the template and have them fill in their own performance targets corresponding to what we've laid out. Then we evaluate them on how well they do what they've said they'll do. We help them, of course. We coach them all along the way to meet—and exceed—their own plan."

Thus is achieved an organization-wide alignment of expectations, efforts, and results—an alignment that expands the meaning of teamwork to include leadership and rank and file alike.

The AT&T Goal Deployment Process typifies AT&T Solutions' democratic management approach.

"Our leadership doesn't stand aloof at the top of a traditional organizational pyramid," says Regional Managing Partner Bob Scheier. "Rick wants to hear from people at all levels. He feels any given person has something to contribute in a given situation. It's like in baseball when you put in a long-ball hitter to go for the fences, or a speedster to steal a base. People are flattered when their special abilities are sought out, and they accept it when they are not. And they're honest when they're put in a situation where they don't feel they can cope. It's situational, and each person has particular weaknesses as well as strengths."

In addition to stimulating innovative ideas, AT&T Solutions' open-door policy and nonhierarchical approach create another valuable workplace commodity—fun.

"Rick's organization is definitely different in terms of pace and speed," says Managing Partner John Damian, "but what's really special is its sense of fun. This is a refreshing place to work."

A leader who generates fun generates everlasting loyalty all through the ranks.

"People who've worked with Rick in the past want to work with him in the future," says Damian. "Including me."

"A good rule of thumb," appends Frank Ianna, "is when it stops being fun, get out, do something different. If it's not fun, it ain't worth it. So far it's worth it with Rick."

High spirits aren't worth anything, of course, without solid business success. To date, however, AT&T Solutions has proved that people who thoroughly enjoy what they are doing achieve the best results.

While progress toward Goal Deployment Process business targets can be documented, and employees' skill and knowledge levels assessed, personal working styles and behaviors must also be considered before the performance picture is fully colored and complete.

However, even in the most humane organizations with the most well-adjusted teams, discussing styles and behavior can be uncomfortable.

No one likes personal criticism, but AT&T Solutions knew that growth can only happen with sheer honesty.

This means positive, constructive criticism, of course, but even this is hard to give, much less take. It's so difficult that many large corporations ignore bad behavior if an employee's business numbers are right.

"In corporate America," Rick says, "behavior takes a back seat to results, and when people consider behavior at all, they think other people have a problem, not themselves."

The business numbers, skills, and knowledge, and personal behavior are equally important and tightly linked.

Why?

Because they all reflect and promote the company's vision and values. They're cultural.

They're part of an enterprise's whole dream and belief, and it's frankly daring to equally weight and align them in a performance review, since doing so runs counter to the traditional performance appraisal approach.

AT&T Solutions uses the image of a three-legged stool to illustrate this point (see Exhibit 6).

If one leg is broken or missing, the stool won't hold any weight—the weight of an important client deal, for instance, which can collapse when any team member lacks even one "leg."

"We're different from corporate AT&T," says John Wood, AT&T Solutions vice president and managing partner. "Over there you might flunk a deal for business, skills and knowledge, or behavioral reasons, and still get promoted. At AT&T Solutions, you've got to score on all three."

In the behavioral realm, this means receiving feedback from all levels of the organization.

"We use 360-degree feedback quite a bit, even though it's sometimes tough to take," says Rick. "As human beings, we naturally expect and accept feedback from authority figures—our parents, our teachers, our bosses—but hearing what colleagues and subordinates think about us can sometimes rub the wrong way."

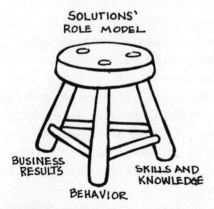

Exhibit 6 The Three Personal Success Factors at
AT&T Solutions

If subordinates' feedback bothers Rick, he handles it very well.

"I was informed by several employees that I was controlling too much decision making too far down the chain. People couldn't get a PC, or they couldn't add a new team member, unless I signed off. They felt oppressed. Their feedback woke me up, and I changed my behavior. And I wouldn't even have known there was a problem if we hadn't been letting these people speak up."

When Rick himself provides feedback to others, the effect is not just corrective, but galvanizing, too.

"Rick is one of the best teachers I've ever seen," declares Wood. "He teaches in a very interesting way—you almost don't realize you're being taught."

Wood cites an instance where Rick spent 20 minutes grilling work team members on their sales strategy and financials. He listened, rebutted some points, listened some more, and made some more comments—most of them hard-hitting and very blunt.

"A lot of people thought he was kicking the crap out of them," says Wood. "It wasn't until later that they realized what they'd learned from what he'd said."

So how did the guy who'd been on the payroll for only three weeks, and who thought he knew financial engineering A to Z, feel after Rick had shredded his presentation?

"He felt pretty beat up," Wood admits, "but he was pretty sure that next time he'd be better prepared."

In AT&T Solutions' overall scheme of in-house communications, performance feedback is just a part.

Because denial and avoidance have no place in healthy teams, private, face-to-face communication is encouraged for settling personal disputes. Rick sometimes referees these sessions. In the toughest disagreements, an arbitrator—often the two disputants' team leader—is brought in.

In AT&T Solutions' early days, when there were fewer personnel, employees would physically gather for "town meetings" to hear about upcoming initiatives and recent deals that had been done.

Today, with 10,000 employees in 60 countries, the town meetings are electronic instead of physical. Led by a top company leader, these interactive Web-cast teleconferences are forums for companywide announcements, discussions, and debate.

"I spend a lot of time communicating to the company's employees and management," says CEO Mike Armstrong. "I send out e-mails—'As I See It,' as I call them—to announce important events. I'm not Abraham Lincoln, but I try to make them clean and clear. I can't touch 150,000 people personally, but through the system I can."

For Armstrong, leadership is an interpersonal challenge.

"I don't believe that you can lead unless you are involved and know what's going on and thus can appreciate the organization's problems, challenges, and demands. I know I'm sometimes criticized for being too hands-on, but unless I'm fully involved, I can't support our people as I should."

Clearly, AT&T Solutions runs very fast because it runs very smart. Part of its brilliance is in treating its employees as precious human beings whose value as team players flows from their value as individual selves.

Says Bill O'Brien, "There's more teamwork here than in most places. Oh, we fight like cats and dogs among ourselves. There's a lot of kicking and screaming and yelling, but there's also rock-solid mutual respect and a collective dedication to results."

In Dick Anderson's opinion, AT&T now shares this belief. "I think Mike has recognized that AT&T Solutions' bold ambitions, our devotion to teamwork, our reward system, and the way we focus on very clear growth targets should be emulated across AT&T."

"For all the technology, our industry is still people based," says Rick. "People are our real value proposition these days. Unfortunately, in the current tight job market, it's hard to attract the best and the brightest, and when you get them, you can't afford to let them go. That's why we invest so much time, money, and effort in training, motivating, and communicating. It helps our people invest in themselves."

"We talk about good goose behavior," says Brian Maloney. "For us, it reflects the AT&T Solutions way of business and of life."

Goose behavior?

"When geese fly, there's a leader for a time," Brian explains. "You see them flying in that perfect 'V,' and if you watch them long enough, the leader will fall out and go to the back, and someone else will move into the leadership position. There's no permanent number one goose, no ruler by divine right." (See Exhibit 7.)

Nor is there at AT&T Solutions, right?

"That's right, and that's why we're not big on titles and levels and strict pecking order."

Exhibit 7 Good Goose Behavior

What else about the geese?

"Well, flying in this V-formation, the noble geese travel thousands of miles with ease and precision. As each bird moves its wings, it creates an uplift for the bird following. Did you know that formation flying is 70 percent more efficient than flying alone?"

Really? 70 percent?

"When one of the great birds falls out of formation, it suddenly feels the drag and resistance of trying to fly alone, and so it quickly rejoins the formation to take advantage of the lifting power of the bird immediately in front."

But the leader doesn't have another bird in front.

"Exactly, and so it tires more quickly than the others, and when it's too tired to lead any longer, it rotates back into the formation and another bird takes its place at the point."

Why do geese honk?

"Each flock finds its own rhythm. The pulsating sound of the great wings beating together excites and energizes the whole formation. The geese honk from behind to encourage those up front to keep their speed up."

And in the autumn, when the hunters come out?

"When a goose is shot—or gets sick—two geese drop out of formation to follow it as it falls. On the ground they stay with it and protect it until it can fly again, or until it dies. Then they launch out on their own to start a new formation, or they catch up with their old flock."

Who are some of AT&T Solutions' other good geese?

We need only gaze skyward at some of their V-formation teams in flight—for example, Glenn Swift's Technology One Alliance team that serves Bank One.

FRANK KRIEG'S STORY

I'm the business director for the AT&T Solutions–IBM–Bank One deal. I'm responsible for the financial aspects, the vendor-supplier relationship, and the relationship with the bank's business people.

Putting together the operating principles was a collaborative effort. The alliance leadership team got together and discussed our vision, and then we got some input from the T1A group. We did the traditional benchmarking and alignment surveys, which showed we were in pretty good shape. Writing up the principles took about four months. In the time since then, except for a few word changes, they've held up.

We have a team member board. Brian Maloney and Rick are on it, along with their counterparts at IBM and the bank. Brian and Rick don't come into meetings with pre-written decrees and fancy charts that they expect us to bless. They sit down and roll up their sleeves and invite everyone to think and make decisions as a group.

ART LOCKE'S STORY

After 13 years deep in the bowels of AT&T, I was very excited to come to AT&T Solutions about two years ago. AT&T had gotten stale for me. I needed some growth and excitement. As the Transformation Executive in the Bank One Technology One Alliance, I've gotten plenty of both.

At AT&T Solutions it's easy to talk to people who can help you get things done. No one here gets offended if you don't go through proper channels. There *are* no proper channels, and so business moves at a faster pace than it does at AT&T. There's more pulling together for common goals, more collective energy, less bureaucratic delay.

Having said that, we do bring the sense of discipline that clients expect from AT&T—and that we need ourselves to run a business that, at a certain level, relies on tight structure and repetition. We just can't be so rigorous that we freeze up.

In the context of our industry, the structure and spirit of our alliance is not a normal one. Most in-house IT staffs treat outsourcers as just vendors and suppliers, whereas we arrive as collaborative part-ners. Some clients and partners have a hard time getting used to that. They're so accustomed to banging on vendors to get what they want.

In swapping out Bank One's telecom infrastructure and upgrading their old network, we disrupted their IT organization. There was a fair amount of confusion and resentment as a result. Some people were unhappy that they'd been transferred; others were unhappy that they weren't. As the leader of the IT transition, my biggest challenge was healing emotional wounds and rebuilding trust. Because the job can't go forward if people are seriously upset.

What sustains us most on this team is Glenn Swift's involving us all in his vision of how the alliance should work. He trusts us to act within the bounds of that understanding, and he empowers us by doing that.

Glenn makes joint accountability a key to success. We're like an orchestra, all of us first-chair players, all playing the same piece.

"Invigorating," is how another Technology One Alliance team member describes her experience working with Glenn Swift.

Says another, "The legacy systems and processes that encumber you at big corporations aren't obstacles here."

Other comments include the following:

"We're a marquee engagement, and we're proud to be an AT&T Solutions engine for growth."

"We're running our own business, we're responsible for our own day-to-day decisions, and we have our own P&L. Though some days you feel this is totally crazy, there's nowhere I'd rather be."

"Glenn is a roll-up-the-sleeves type of manager. He's our biggest critic and our biggest cheerleader, too. He embodies respect—for both the company and the individual. And he instills that respect in all of us."

The Textron engagement team members are unanimous in praising their own AT&T Solutions leader, Rob Vatter.

"He's dynamic," one says.

"He's not a micromanager," another adds. "He lets you do what you want."

"He'll take risks."

"He's decisive."

"Customer satisfaction is his major drive."

"He's not obsessed with getting approvals from Florham Park."

"He puts us all in positions where the client can see our talents and skills. That's empowering for us."

Chase Manhattan team leader Russ Fairchild empowers his team members, too.

"He's great at giving us support," says one Fairchild loyalist. "He's our anchor, but he makes us accountable and lets us make a lot of decisions on our own."

Says another Chase team member, "When we're with Russ in client interactions, he supports any decisions we make."

Sal Lipari manages the AT&T Solutions team for Merrill Lynch.

"As the business here has grown, Sal has given me the opportunity to grow, too," one team member says.

Another commented, "Together, we run this as our own business, we all have our own P&L, and we're accountable for what we do."

Another person declares, "We're high achievers here, but we never stop using our resources, including each other, to learn and grow."

Helping each other learn and develop—and keeping the company in high-flying V-formation—is what AT&T Solutions teamwork is all about. As Bill Blinn notes, most professional services put their employees on an "up or out" career track. "At AT&T Solutions, we say, 'Grow or go.'"

"It's a spirit as much as anything," says John Damian, "a sort of one-for-all-and-all-for-one approach to engagements that are highly customized, so everything stays fresh."

Now AT&T Solutions' big challenge will be keeping the vision and the spirit fresh as the company grows larger and more successful, and as the race for excellence heats up.

DEBRIEFING

Quintessential Teams

The Noun

In their book *Virtual Teams*, Lipnack and Stamps describe teams that work "across space, time, and organizational boundaries, with links strengthened by webs of technology."[3]

Team AT&T Solutions works like that, and is a virtual team in that regard—but it's also more than that.

It's quintessential.

What is its quintessence?

A general definition from *The Random House College Dictionary* first:

quintessence, n., 1. the pure and concentrated essence of a substance. 2. the most perfect embodiment of something. 3. (in ancient and medieval philosophy) the fifth essence or element, ether, supposed to be the constituent matter of the heavenly bodies, the others being air, water, fire, and earth.

How do AT&T Solutions teams fit those definitions?

More importantly at this point, how can your teams fit the definitions?

Quintessential teams—we'll call them QTs—are virtual teams that also have the following traits:

- Highly and quickly adaptive
- Inclusive in their membership, embracing their own members plus customers, partners, and competitors, too
- Geared to run at the speed of change

What serious evaluative efforts have you made in your teams? Are they concentrated embodiments of virtually quintessential—or quintessentially virtual—working groups?

In business terms, are they as elementally constituent as air, water, fire, and earth?

AT&T Solutions' teams are.

Here's how yours can be, too.

The Verbs

Establish Project- or Process-Focused QTs

The biggest problem facing teams today just might be their habit of focusing internally.

Lynn Brown says HR teams are often guilty of doing that. "Most HR functions are 90 percent internally focused," she remarks. "But the good ones, like ours, interface with the clients from day one."

Quintessential teams look outward instead of in, making customers, partners, competitors, and their own functional support specialists active members of the overall group. Contemplating one's own navel is impossible when solving customers' problems is job one.

Co-locate to Be Customer-Intimate

"Location, location, location" is the real estate agents' favorite pitch.

"Co-location, co-location, co-location" should be yours.

To be customer-intimate, professional consulting firms should spend 90 percent of their time at their clients' places of work. Manufacturing process teams should be at their clients' facilities a similar amount of time. Outsourcers to retailers should set up shop at their clients' stores.

How much time you spend on site with your clients depends on your particular type of work. But it's probably more time than you would initially think.

AT&T Solutions' projects are called engagements because they *engage* clients in an intellectual, emotional, and also a physical sense. Instead of communicating just by phone, e-mail, and fax, AT&T Solutions' teams literally work shoulder-to-shoulder with clients on the clients' home turf.

At the same time, AT&T Solutions provides clients with work space at its home offices, making co-location a two-way street.

In outsourcing, proximity raises productivity and profitability. That's not a theory; that's a fact.

Think of it this way: You can't dance with a partner who's standing four feet away.

Breed Confidence with Confidence

Rick tells this story:

> We were in Ohio negotiating the $2 billion Bank One agreement. We were almost through, but then the bank handed us a list of requests that we had to accept if we wanted to close the deal. Each request had a financial hit, so the AT&T Solutions team took a break to discuss the situation. On our team was a young guy in his twenties, two years out of college, a likely future CFO. I asked him what we should do. I didn't ask for his general input, I asked him point-blank: Should we say yes to the requests and give up some earnings or should we walk away from the deal?
>
> I'll never forget his look. It said, "What? You're asking *me*?" I repeated my question: "What would you do in my place?"
>
> His eyes were half-a-mile wide, but after a moment he got over his shock and said we should take the deal. He said we should agree to the requests, because this was too big a contract to pass up. And he was right; it was too big to miss. He gave me the right advice.

What's Rick's point?

That people are flattered by confidence and trust.

That they rise to critical challenges rather than shrink away from them.

That if you give them a bat in the ninth inning with two down and a runner on third and the team a run behind, they'll knock one out of the park.

Or they'll poke one through the infield for the tying tally.

Or if they strike out they'll go down swinging, and they'll be better hitters next time up.

Rick knows that because he's not just a businessman, he's a brilliant coach.

Create a Fail Forward Fast Culture

As a team, evaluate your pace.

Who are your most powerful drivers for speed? Customers? Competitors? Owners? Yourselves?

How can you stay on the front lines of the new economy and build your future together?

Create a Schedule Cop

The only speed in the new economy is full speed ahead.

The only speed limit is how fast you can go (and then add 90 mph).

Designate one person to keep all team members in the far-left passing lane, and to fine those who aren't driving fast enough.

Remember, most deadlines are yesterday—or the day before that.

Give QTs Their Own Place to Work

Sometimes we all want to go into our own rooms and shut the door on the world.

QTs do, too.

They want to hold private meetings, exchange information, connect to the Web, review scheduling, or just have fun as a group.

Quintessential teams thrive in the air, water, fire, and earth—but they also need rooms of their own.

Find New Ways to Have Fun

Laser tag after a tough negotiating session

Karaoke after a team performance review

Cater baby back ribs to celebrate exceeding this year's business targets

The team that plays together stays together.

Enough said.

8

Staying a Winner through Vision and Innovation

S*ETTING*: *A large conference room at AT&T Solutions' headquarters in Florham Park, New Jersey. Rick Roscitt is sitting with four new hires: Linda Martin, Elizabeth Reilly, Jack Kershaw, and Paul Fazio. Earlier today, Rick gave his formal presentation to all new hires regarding AT&T Solutions' history, vision, and cultural values. Now, as evening falls, Rick remains, chatting informally with these four new AT&T Solutions employees.*

Through the window, a brilliant crimson sunset is fading to purple-gray. The light reflects off the windshields of the cars in the AT&T Solutions parking lot, which is still two-thirds full.

Rick refills Jack's coffee mug from a freshly brewed pot.

Jack: You say you started out in a conference room with 12 people and now you're 10,000 . . .

Rick: Actually, we're 10,004 counting each of you.

Jack: But back then, when you looked into the future, did you see your-selves growing this big this fast?

Rick: We saw it as a possibility. We dreamed it could happen. And we believed that the dream could come true.

Jack: How did you start believing? I mean from day one in that room.

Rick: We talked and argued and shaped our vision of who we wanted to · be.

Jack: But to think you could succeed like this, before you'd had your first success—that was a pretty big leap of faith.

Rick: It was easier coming from nothing, and we liked it that way. We didn't have to remake an existing vision. We could start from scratch. Look at this piece of paper. (Rick tears a blank sheet from his notepad.) What do you see on it?

Jack: Nothing.

Elizabeth: Or anything. You can write whatever you want.

Rick: Good, go ahead! (Rick hands her a pencil. She hesitates.) Or bet-ter, draw something. Look out the window, draw what you see.

Elizabeth: I can't see much out there, it's pretty dark.

Rick: Then we'll make the sun come up. (Rick draws a rudimentary horizon with a radiant sunrise, then holds up the sheet.) This is basi-cally what we did, the 12 of us in that conference room: we drew a rising sun on a blank sheet of paper. And then we filled in the bushes, the people, and the trees. We didn't look out the window because it was AT&T's window, so we made our own window. We didn't replicate a reality that already existed. We drew our own to please ourselves. It wasn't art yet, but it was a vision—even if the vision wasn't the same as corporate AT&T's.

Jack: And when the AT&T people didn't buy your vision right away?

Rick: Some of them did, some didn't.

Linda: How did you cope with that?

Rick: We didn't rub their noses in it. We didn't tell them this is the way the world has to look from now on. Instead, we stayed true to our vision, and acted in accordance with it. We didn't preach behavior, we modeled it. That began to appeal to some people, especially when we started having success.

Paul: What was the turning point?

Rick: There was no magic moment when everyone jumped on board. A few did at a time, then a few more hopped on, and after awhile, it became an acceptable—even an exciting thing to do. And so we grew.

Jack: But you lost some people along the way.

Rick: We did—the ones who couldn't share the vision, who felt themselves more important than the team. Heck, when I joined AT&T, I thought I'd be a really big shot, I'd be the center of attention in whatever department, everyone would answer to me. But then I learned that the key isn't holding responsibility, it's sharing it. You can see much more through many pairs of eyes than just your own two.

Elizabeth: But some people see better than others. How do you factor for that?

Rick: You're right, some people can see a pattern with just one dot. Others need four, five, or six dots, and some need many more. To speed up everyone seeing the pattern together, one person has to spot it early and shout, "Land ho!" Then everybody all at once— employees, clients, and shareholders—can see the same thing.

Linda: But today, with so many eyes at AT&T Solutions, doesn't the vision sometimes get blurred?

Rick: Sometimes it does. And sometimes I worry that we'll lose our bearings as we become a bigger and bigger part of AT&T, and that we'll lose our maverick streak. Because it's tough staying true to our founding vision while we're increasingly beholden to the corporation's shareholders. We're not a clean sheet of paper anymore.

Paul: So how does AT&T Solutions keep its bearings?

Rick: We reconfirm our values and our culture. We refocus our vision. We remember how we dared ourselves to start this crazy journey, and then we dare ourselves to stay on this precarious high and winding mountain road.

Jack: The company stays hungry, you mean; it takes new risks.

Rick: Right! Risks are exciting. They capture the imagination, and they inspire harder work. If I say hey, everybody, take a deep breath and follow me on a bold journey—around the block—even twice—what's the thrill in that? That's the low-risk, low-reward approach: You stay out of trouble, but you don't accomplish very much. Instead, we say let's climb Mount Everest.

Paul: And then swim the Atlantic after lunch.

Rick: And the Pacific after that. Tell me, why did each of you join AT&T Solutions?

Linda: The challenge. The chance to do something really meaningful.

Paul: To have a personal stake in a company's success. To be recognized for good work.

Jack: I wanted to join a start-up, but not a little one. AT&T Solutions combined pioneering spirit and real business clout.

Rick: So you didn't come just for the money.

Elizabeth: We could make the same money across the street.

Paul: A little more money two blocks down!

Jack: Really? Where? At what address?

Rick: The point is you've got to stick to your vision and see it through. Walt Disney put it this way . . .

Linda: Dream, Believe, Dare, Do.

Rick: Correct. Where'd you learn that?

Linda: In a book—which also quoted Walt as saying, "You don't build the product for yourself, you need to know what the people want and build it for them."

Rick: Walt was right. The trouble is, people want more and more these days, and faster and faster, too. It's a strain to keep pace with client demands, much less stay a jump ahead. If you don't put a premium on innovation, you're dead. If innovation isn't a prime company value, if it's not at the core of the culture, then your vision will just be a pretty picture, it won't work.

Elizabeth: What drives innovation these days, the end user clients or the innovators themselves?

Rick: Both do. Chase pushed us right at the start; then McDermott rammed us into high gear. Each of those clients shaped us as much as we shaped them. From those experiences we learned not just to listen to customers, but also to say yes to them. At the same time, we keep growing and developing our people, processes, and tools on our own. We don't wait till we're nudged. We continuously enlarge our knowledge base so we're ready to meet any new challenge when it comes. We're always saying, "We don't know enough yet." And the fact is, we'll never know enough—knowledge is expanding too fast. There's too much to know! And since networking is largely to blame for that, we're both victim and beneficiary of our own success.

Paul: On that point, how does AT&T Solutions balance implementing what's new today and developing what'll be hot next week?

Rick: It's the short-term, long-term juggling act. If we blow it, we and our clients get stuck with technology that, by the time it's implemented, is obsolete. But we can't just sit and wait for what's coming down the road in six months. We've got to strategize and act with what we know and what we've got, plus what we're able to predict. So we say to clients: "Here's where you've been, here's where you can go in the near-term, and here's where we can help you arrive farther down the road. Now, how fast do you want to move? Do you need a quick return? How's your tolerance for longer-term results?" Since we're good at reading the industry tea leaves, we can help them make their decisions. We can offer them insights from AT&T Labs and our innovative partners like Cisco and IBM.

Elizabeth: So clients depend on AT&T Solutions in making their own internal decisions about technological growth.

Rick: We're mission critical to them. That's a huge step forward when you consider that networking was ignored or considered a necessary evil once upon a time. In some companies it used to be that the telecommunications networking person sat next to the janitor. The only difference was that the chairman knew the janitor (he called him to fix something in his office from time to time), and he never talked to the networking guy in his life. Now networking is so important, it's outsourced. Of course, outsourcing creates a whole new level of risk for the customer, who doesn't want to tell his board, "We just bought the cure for our ills," and then, 18 months later, have to say, "The old cure doesn't work any more, we need new pills." We help clients out of this bind, and we show how we can morph their platform over time to keep it up to date. We help them balance innovation with its inherent risk.

Linda: What about AT&T Solutions' clients being nudged toward innovation by their own customers?

Rick: Merrill Lynch is a good example of that. They had no use for online trading at first, and they'd have outlawed it if they could. "Investing should be broker based," they said. "Online trading is taking your family funds to Las Vegas. We won't be a part of that!" Also, they just weren't ready for it. They weren't technologically set up. But customers wouldn't be denied—not just individual traders but large ones, as well. Firms like Schwab and E*Trade and Ameritrade had turned up the heat. So Merrill faced stepping up to online technology or losing its customer base. That's when they came to us. And that's when innovation becomes not just a two-way, but a three-way street. In helping Merrill to innovate, we were nudged to innovate, too—by the innovation of Cisco, our technology partner, which had upgraded a key component. We had to solve customizing it for the Merrill application in three months! We did, of course, and now Merrill is the second largest volume online trader in the world, and they're still growing fast.

Paul: Merrill didn't just change its technology, it changed its business model, too.

Rick: You're exactly right. And not just by going online, but by blending online trading and broker contact. Customers can phone their Merrill brokers for advice before independently keying in what they want to do. Their online trades are reflected in their overall portfolios. It's the best of both worlds for Merrill and its customers alike.

Elizabeth: We forget that a lot of companies were afraid of the Internet at first.

Rick: Hey, once upon a time people shouted, "Get a horse," when they saw a Model-T.

Jack: Has AT&T Solutions innovated in its own business models?

Rick: You bet. Our whole cultural notion of working less as individuals than as members of engagement teams while often serving on multiple cross-functional groups—that's new in the industry. Teamwork toward winning and undertaking engagements prevents the skirmishes between accounting and sales and operations that often crop up in big companies with silo mentalities. And the idea that AT&T Solutions doesn't invade a client's space, but becomes a part of it— actually merges with the client's staff—that's a twist on the outsourcing model. We make ourselves a virtual extension of the client's corporation. We're not AT&T Solutions anymore; we're part of Merrill, part of Textron, and part of Bank One.

Linda: Maybe we should call our work "insourcing."

Rick: We should. We tried "life-cycle management" and some other alternative terms once, but none stuck. So we're still outsourcers, but we're actually more than that.

Jack: How are engagement teams led?

Rick: We're innovating there, too. The general manager of an engagement is in place during its whole life cycle. It could be 5 years, or it could be 10. Our relationship with the client remains stable that way. And we tell our general managers, "This is your show, it's your business, so run it as such." And sometimes they come back to me and say, "Can I add more people?" And I say, "Look at your income statement, can you afford more people, will they add value? Make the decision yourself." Because you can't tell GMs to build engagements around P&Ls and balance sheets, and to motivate their people, and to grow their businesses to the next level—and not let them make their own decisions! You've got to turn them loose! Tap their creativity! Inspire a sense of accountability and responsibility! Make them realize, hey, I'm out here on the edge, I've got to innovate in my own job to make this work! The rest of AT&T doesn't operate this way. Ours is a different model. It's innovation to make our insourcing brand of outsourcing work.

Linda: As a leading innovator, how does AT&T Solutions keep the creative furnaces stoked? On a personal level, that is.

Rick: You quoted Walt Disney a moment ago. I understand the Disney company runs a "Gong Show" exercise, where anyone from any level can pitch an idea to the CEO. Some Disney movies and Disney World attractions have actually come out of that. We don't have a "Gong Show," but we do have our electronic town meetings, and a Web page where people can post suggestions. And we read them, every one. And anyone can e-mail me directly, or get me or other managers on the phone. Hey, if any of you has an idea right now, speak up!

Elizabeth: Give us a week.

Rick: In my mind, face-to-face contact can't be beat. I catch people first thing in the morning, or in the hallway on a break. I ask them what they're working on, and it's amazing how people open up. And I usually end up calling one of my other managers and saying, "Wow, you know what I just heard? Let's give this idea some support!"

(Outside, a full moon can be seen rising in the sky. Paul stands up to stretch.)

Rick: Should I make another pot of coffee?

Paul: Decaf for me.

Rick: Anyone who wants to head home, go ahead, it's 7 o'clock.

Jack: Only 7? I thought that's when the AT&T Solutions workday just gets started.

Paul: On second thought, I'll take caffeinated.

Elizabeth: Same for me.

Rick: Linda?

Linda: Sure, caffeinated. No cream. Two sugars. The night is young.

DEBRIEFING

Predictable Problems/Failing Forward Fast

When some people see a mountain, they think only of getting over it to reach the gentler, low-lying terrain on the other side.

When people at AT&T Solutions see a mountain, they think only of getting to the top. They always keep the peak in sight.

Mountain climbing in business is as hazardous as it is in the Himalayas or the Alps. But Rick asserts that "risks are exciting, they capture the imagination, they inspire harder work."

Do the risks merit courting the predictable problems of steep, icy slopes and the dangers of failing forward (and falling downward) fast?

Let's bivouac for a moment and assess both the perils and the rewards of making any risky ascent.

The Noun

Why treat predictable problems together with failing forward fast?

Because problems and failure are both unwanted events.

They're unwanted, that is, until you realize how beneficial they can be.

The fact is, there will always be problems and failure. So don't just get used to them—instead, use them to positive effect.

How can you do that?

By constantly looking ahead, anticipating trouble instead of letting it hit you from your blind side.

By treating missteps as strides in the right direction, instead of detours that waste precious time.

As John Chambers said, "I don't want to do five perfect deals; I want to do ten knowing that eight will succeed and two will fail. Because I learn more from failure than success."

If Columbus hadn't sailed west from Portugal, we might still think the world was flat.

If Rick Roscitt hadn't hatched AT&T Solutions, AT&T might still be getting together its networking outsourcing act.

Intrepid mariners and pioneering entrepreneurs don't have all the maps. They chart their course by the stars in the sky. They forecast the weather with meteorological instruments as well by the feeling in their bones. They steer clear of tempests, but sometimes get caught in driving rain. If their ships are swamped, they bail them out—then continue sailing on to port.

Leading at the speed of change means examining the failure, then quickly getting beyond it to reap in the thrill of victory.

The Verbs

Identify Potential Barriers to Success

At least once each quarter, meet with your team to scan the road ahead for impediments that might block the way to your desired results.

If possible, meet for the same purpose with your customers, too.

Clear the Road to Results

After spotting the impediments, send your team members back to their regular jobs and clear the debris yourself.

Why shouldn't your colleagues help you?

Because a leader at the speed of change stays out ahead of the troops.

And, if your team is with you out on the road, there's no one minding the store.

Celebrate Failure

Failure is a bad word for those who seek stability, but it is a prime motivator for companies like AT&T Solutions, Disney, and ADC.

One of the messages of *Leading at the Speed of Change* is this: You've got to Fail at the Speed of Change, too!

And when you do, rejoice! You've blundered through a door which, had you played it safe, would have remained forever closed. Beyond the door may lie a sumptuous realm, hidden to those who never dared to make mistakes.

Or it may be an airshaft or a wall of bricks, you never know. It doesn't matter: you can chalk it up to experience, which is valuable in itself, since the wider the range of your experience, the closer you are to your goal.

We admit, it's counter-instinctive for people to accept failure, much less court it by taking risks.

So make failure a goal in itself.

How?

Try this: Give a prize for the dumbest mistake of the month.

(Then don't be surprised if the lesson it teaches triggers some major success.)

It's better that team members ask forgiveness for errors than beg permission just to try.

Don't forget that the first steamboat was initially dubbed "Fulton's Folly."

Develop Processes or Guidelines

Sir Isaac Newton wrote, "If I have seen further, it is by standing on the shoulders of giants."

We all stand on giants' shoulders, and we should enjoy the view. But we should also strive to be giants ourselves, and let our shoulders be our colleagues' and successors' vantage points.

Newton didn't just gaze far ahead; he developed principles that framed what he beheld.

That is what we should do with our insights: frame them so they are available and accessible to others who may then deepen the focus and expand the point of view.

We should steal more from each other, as AT&T Solutions' VP for Human Resources Lynn Brown has said. We shouldn't redo what other people have already done. We shouldn't rewrite already-written books. We should unashamedly use other employees' ideas and leverage them to full advantage.

Why should we do that?

As Lynn explained, "We'll save time that way, and time is money. We'll lower our expenses and keep our margins up."

Good reasons, we'd have to say.

And having said that, we'll add that not all work should be copied. Not all previous insights are true. Paradigms are not gospel just by dint of being venerable. They can be updated, revised, or thrown out. Encourage your teams to challenge and modify processes and guidelines as they see fit, because every customized solution demands a customized working approach.

PART
IV

Do

Winning at Home: The Roar of the Crowd

Instead of actually making sneakers, Nike makes advertising slogans that exhort us to drive to the hoop with the game on the line—wearing the "swoosh," of course, and pumped up by the roar of the home crowd.

"Just Do It," Nike says—and "Just Do It" is effectively what AT&T Solutions now says to itself as it completes its first five years of dreaming, believing, and daring.

With the home crowd roaring, AT&T Solutions takes the outlet pass, drives the lane, and slam-dunks.

Of course, those who "just do it" find that doing it once encourages a demand for encores. "What have you done for me lately?" becomes the refrain of clients, partners, and shareholders, who are not so much fickle as addicted to home team victories.

For this rabid gallery, and for its own pride and profits, AT&T Solutions comes through in the clutch, inscribing client after client on its massive headquarters lobby wall (see Exhibit 8), which it calls its "Wall of Wins." The victories aren't AT&T Solutions' alone, though—the clients share in them as well.

Exhibit 8 The Wall of Wins at AT&T Solutions

This is not just a client roster; it's an American business Hall of Fame, and AT&T Solutions helps all its inductees stay enshrined.

Unlike most halls of fame, though, whose members are long since retired or deceased, this one's honorees are still active and—with AT&T Solutions' help—are setting new records every day.

"I've been there at the Wall when every new client name has gone up," says Patrick O'Malley. "Each time is a thrill because each client is an honored contributor to our growing success. We mean that. After all, we're not some giant company that can afford to be complacent and sit back. We're growing one client at a time, and our aim is to help our clients succeed and grow, too. We want to exceed their expectations. We want to make each client feel that working with us is the best thing they ever did."

For most companies, AT&T Solutions' exposure of the hidden costs of business is a revelation. "Most organizations have never had to capture the true financial cost of their operation because it's broken up by divisions," states Rick. "It's obscured because it's fragmented, but we know where to look. When we add it up for them in terms of moving functionality across the line, the hidden costs are dramatically revealed and the business-case requirement shifts. Then we help them look forward and project transition costs. 'Over the next three years,' we say to them, 'where do you want to go? Do you see a competitor who's set to aggressively attack your turf? If so, let's meet the assault, let's put together a business case and go forward. The return on your investment will be very great.'"

AT&T Solutions' best source of growth has been its existing customer base. Limited initial contracts have allowed room for expanded commitments as these clients have bulked up.

Says Rick, "If you give your customers what you promise, and then a bit more, and you stand with them through growth, then you'll probably be given the first shot at new work that comes up."

Remember AT&T Solutions' trial by fire at McDermott? After gaining this client's initial thumbs-up in 1995, Rick and his team earned an even bigger share of its business later on:

FOR RELEASE WEDNESDAY, MARCH 31, 1999
AT&T WINS CONTRACT WORTH ABOUT
$60 MILLION A YEAR FOR 10 YEARS
TO MANAGE McDERMOTT GLOBAL IT

"We run their servers now, we run their LANs and their WANs, we run their software applications," says Rick, "and we run everything they've got worldwide. And the reason we do is we stuck with them early when the going was tough."

Naturally, potential clients regard a company's past and current performance as a predictor of future success. Having an existing client like McDermott renew and significantly expand its agreement therefore gave AT&T Solutions' standing in the marketplace a huge boost.

For its part, McDermott sought a quantum boost in its customer service capabilities. Said Roger Tetrault, McDermott's chairman of the board and CEO, "This contract supports our corporate goals, puts our IT needs into highly capable hands, and creates an environment that offers expanded opportunities to our IT employees."[1]

For 280 McDermott professionals, those opportunities included becoming employees of AT&T Solutions.

The enhanced working relationship made even greater use of the AT&T Solutions Global Client Support Center in Durham, North Carolina.

Said Rick, "Our GCSC will assure that users can connect to the business information and applications they need anytime, anywhere via the McDermott global networking platform, rendering the physical location of the applications irrelevant."

Another early client to deepen its involvement with AT&T Solutions was Merrill Lynch:

FOR RELEASE MONDAY, OCTOBER 18, 1999
 EXODUS, AT&T SOLUTIONS COLLABORATE FOR MERRILL LYNCH ONLINE (MLOL)
  Exodus Communications™, Inc., a leader in complex Internet hosting and managed services, and AT&T today announced that Merrill Lynch & Co., Inc., one of the world's leading financial management and advisory companies, has chosen Exodus™ and AT&T Solutions to provide state-of-the-art hosting facilities and professional and network management services for Merrill Lynch's Web-based investment offerings.

In addition to expanding an existing AT&T Solutions client contract, this deal brought AT&T Solutions a new technology partner, too.

"Merrill Lynch's evolution to e-business and our collaboration with Exodus are natural extensions of our relationship," said Rick.

John McKinley, Merrill Lynch's senior vice president and chief technology officer, commented, "Exodus's professional expertise in hosting extensive Internet operations and the e-business networking prowess of AT&T Solutions are significant advantages that will support our mission-critical Internet operations."

These operations were mission critical, indeed. According to Forrester Research, 9.7 million households would be trading online by 2002 and would have $3 trillion in Internet brokerage accounts, or approximately one-fifth of all retail investment assets. Such a vast, burgeoning market could not be passed up.

For Exodus, the collaboration with AT&T Solutions was mission critical, too.

"We are pleased to be working with AT&T Solutions in support of Merrill Lynch as it launches a new era in online investing," announced Ellen M. Hancock, Exodus's president and CEO. "It is our goal to deliver reliability and scalability to MLOL, both of which are vital to accommodate the growth of its online community."[2]

For AT&T Solutions, the deal sweetened its Merrill Lynch association, which had been bearing rich fruit since its formation in 1996.

"We are a virtual extension of the Merrill Lynch team, providing design, engineering, implementation, and management of their global networking capabilities," said Rick.

Those capabilities now included a "Trusted Global Advisor" platform that automated real-time delivery of Merrill Lynch research, market data, and portfolio information, and provided Merrill Lynch's financial consultants with more powerful financial planning tools. Now, individual customers had nearly the same access to information as institutional investors and could make financial decisions much more flexibly and conveniently than before.

In the new networking-centric age, AT&T Solutions was boosting Merrill Lynch to levels of customer-centric service—or better, customer-intimate service—that had never before been reached.

Meanwhile, the AT&T Solutions–Bank One–IBM alliance hadn't been standing still:

FOR RELEASE WEDNESDAY, AUGUST 11, 1999
BANK ONE EXPANDS TECHNOLOGY ONE
ALLIANCE WITH AT&T AND IBM
Awards Additional Contracts Totaling More than $600 Million

"This unique alliance among three industry leaders has already delivered value to the bank's customers and shareholders by strengthening our technology infrastructure and allowing us to deliver products to the market more quickly and at industry benchmark unit costs," said Bank One CIO Marv Adams. "We expect to be able to deliver even more value by extending the scope of the Technology One Alliance across our whole corporation."[3]

AT&T Solutions' new, $465 million mandate was to unify Bank One's data- and voice-networking infrastructure. This contract would run concurrently with the six-year, $1.4 billion agreement that AT&T Solutions had signed with the bank in 1998.

Simultaneously, Bank One paid IBM Global Services an additional $168 million for expanded data center operations, including helpdesk support and management of the bank's mainframe computers and midrange servers.

The migration of over 300 Bank One voice, data, and computing specialists to IBM, AT&T Solutions, and AT&T Solutions' subcontractor Lucent Technologies tightened the Alliance another notch.

In addition to cross-fertilizing and enriching existing business, AT&T Solutions was sowing, cultivating, and harvesting a bumper new crop.

For J.P. Morgan, AT&T Solutions partnered with Computer Sciences Corporation, Andersen Consulting, and Bell Atlantic Network Integration to manage parts of the bank's global technology infrastructure. AT&T Solutions concentrated on the global network operations management.

"Technology is critical to J.P. Morgan's success," said Morgan chairman Douglas A. Warner II, "so critical, and on so many specialized, fast-developing fronts, that no one firm can be a leader in all of them. Teaming up with these firms will put us at the forefront of creative, flexible management of technology, increasing our ability to exploit new technologies, manage costs, and create competitive advantage."

Added Peter A. Miller, the bank's co-head of Corporate Technology, "It will free up our internal technologists to focus on strategies and innovations that give Morgan a competitive edge."

A year later, J.P. Morgan reported savings of $28 million, meaning the bank spent $322 million during the alliance's first year, as opposed to $350 million in the year before that—a reduction of 8 percent.

A $1.1 billion, 10-year contract with Textron Inc. came next.

"To be among the world's largest and best-performing multi-industry companies, Textron must be able to rapidly deploy telecommunications technology cost-effectively across the entire enterprise," said William Gauld, Textron's CIO and vice president of corporate information management.

Textron, maker of Bell Helicopters, E-Z-Go golf carts, and Cessna airplanes, had their own technologically qualified personnel but feared that their IT department might get sucked into network management as a full-time job. The company was also seeking the kind of global telecom capability that would support its strategy of international acquisitions.[4]

Overall, Textron sought to generate more than 85 percent of its sales from international markets within four years and save over $125 million—or 11 percent—in network management costs within 10 years.

AT&T Solutions was chosen to help in this effort because, according to Gauld, "They share our vision of building a very flexible, predictive infrastructure that will enable us to link globally dispersed multi-industry divisions, electronically connect with our worldwide customers, and respond to the new business opportunities that electronic commerce offers."

The fact that AT&T Solutions was part of AT&T didn't hurt either.

As Textron's current SVP and CIO Ken Bohlen recalls, "AT&T was a leader in telecommunications. Plus, after the deregulation and the split-up, their business model had changed. They were hungry now; they were aggressive in day-to-day operations. So we entered this relationship feeling that we'd both be working hard to drive down costs through more effective and efficient business processes."

AT&T Solutions' contract with Textron defined three primary activities:

1. The acquisition and consolidation of Textron's existing network environment, with improved quality-of-service levels.
2. The planning and deployment of next-generation technologies to meet Textron's strategic and operational requirements.
3. The ongoing support, management, and reassessment of the networking environment and its alignment with Textron's business needs.[5]

Said Rick, "Networking-enabled electronic commerce is no longer something that is 'nice to do'—it's becoming a survival issue. By creating an infrastructure capable of supporting electronic commerce, Textron will transform its business and outpace the competition."

AT&T Solutions' own competition for the engagement was London-based British Telecom, which was ultimately rejected as being ill positioned to handle Textron's large presence in North America.

"British Telecom couldn't support us domestically," William Gauld said.

The road to a solid, long-term relationship with Textron took several twists and turns.

Engagement team leader Rob Vatter explains: "Textron is structured as a holding company. There are five primary segments: aircraft, automotive, corporate, finance, and industrial products. Each segment is responsible for delivering operating profit to the corporation month by month. At first, our outsourcing function was established as a corporate function, and so the divisions had to give up a lot of control. They didn't like that, and they put up resistance. Ultimately, we saw the light and started working directly with the segments, addressing their needs at both a business and IT level. Instead of centering our efforts at Textron corporate headquarters, we got on planes and flew out to Wichita, Dallas, and Detroit. That did the trick."

Another win for the AT&T Solutions home team. Another roar from the home crowd.

And a great victory for Textron, too, as savings have exactly matched the hoped-for 11 percent.

Ken Bohlen says that outsourcing in general—and with AT&T Solutions in particular—is the only way to go. "With the paradigm shift in American industry, you no longer need to own everything inside your four walls. In the new Internet environment there is a tremendous need for speed. So, instead of looking at the win-lose partnerships of the past, you want to link with an organization that becomes a virtual extension of your own. AT&T Solutions has been that organization for us."

From AT&T Solutions' perspective, Bob Hilkin, business manager, says, "It is unique that we can become part of the client's business and work at their own desired pace—while not being subject to the standard regulations of AT&T. If we're successful, it's because of our own efforts: We run the show."

With a subsequent contract to build and operate an enterprisewide networking platform for United Health Group, AT&T Solutions was truly on a roll. The platform bonded more than 30,000 users at the client's service centers, field offices, external vendor sites, and other locations across the United States. The rapid deployment covered more than 300 sites nationwide in 12 months.

AT&T Solutions managed the project from its GCSC in North Carolina and provided on-site support teams to work directly with United Health Group's staff on overall planning, execution, and ongoing operations.

"Networking is enabling technology that allows United Healthcare to communicate beyond traditional corporate walls to conduct business with health care providers, members, and employers using our network for electronic commerce," said the company's CIO Paul LeFort. "To accomplish this mission-critical effort, we've joined forces with AT&T Solutions because of their networking expertise and broad vision of how technology can be used to support our specific business objectives."

The publishing industry soon perceived the benefits of network out-sourcing, too.

In 1998, The McGraw-Hill Companies contracted AT&T Solutions to manage their electronic product delivery network.

Under a seven-year agreement, McGraw-Hill's three main business segments—Financial Services, Educational and Professional Publishing, and Information and Media Services—maintained autonomy in designing their own product-delivery frameworks while integrating their technologies in a corporationwide system that was as seamless as it was high-speed.

The arrangement empowered each unit to

- Integrate electronic products and data across business segments
- Cross-sell its own products and those of other business segments
- Package products around a unified, branded segment image and deliver them over a single network connection
- Tailor products to individual customers' needs
- Partner with complementary content providers
- Accelerate the timeliness of products through online and, in some cases, real-time delivery
- Reduce printing and distribution costs through electronic distribution over a cost-effective, shared global platform

AT&T Solutions also undertook the management of The McGraw-Hill Companies' corporationwide administrative network supporting the day-to-day intranet, e-mail, and administrative functions of its 15,700 employees around the world.

"The network architecture will allow The McGraw-Hill Companies to pinpoint which services are delivered to which customers, and to do that on a large-scale, electronic-commerce basis," said Rick. "The new network will also allow us to monitor service levels with great precision."

Harold McGraw III, chairman, president, and CEO of The McGraw-Hill Companies, had this to say: "By outsourcing network management, we will have all the benefits of owning a state-of-the-art networking platform, but without the vast capital investment required to build and manage it."

He added, "We are excited about our strategic alliance with AT&T, which gives us access to AT&T Solutions' unparalleled networking expertise and brings us to our goal of establishing a global, company-wide product distribution platform for our rich storehouse of brands."[6]

AT&T Solutions had always been a favorite of financial institutions. Now Citibank was considering network outsourcing and perhaps becoming AT&T Solutions' number one banking fan.

Wait a minute—Citibank outsourcing technology? After 30 years of generating breakthrough banking technologies such as branchwide ATM networks, credit card authorization systems, electronic payments networks, and transaction processing systems?

After training many of the day's leading financial technologists, such as its own chairman and CEO John S. Reed?

After Walter Wriston used in-house technical prowess, proprietary technologies, and technology-driven business strategies to build one of the preeminent banks in the world?

Yes.

But why?

"We had things centralized in the mid-1970s, and this structure continued for 20 years," recalls DuWayne Peterson, a former Citibank technologist who later became executive vice president of operations, systems, and telecommunications at Merrill Lynch. But beginning in 1995, Peterson notes, Citibank "realized they were losing economies of scale, spending too much money managing their own databases and business process technologies."[7]

In order to focus on its core banking competencies and to reduce its $1.8 billion annual technology expenditures, which were the highest in the industry at that date, Citibank began dismantling and decentralizing its technology functions.

In 1996 it signed outsourcing agreements with Digital Equipment Corp. and Electronic Data Systems for $500 million and $250 million, respectively. The deals netted Citibank hardware, software, and networking technologies to link 2000 local area data networks and 6000 desktop PCs.

In 1997 Citibank ceased making its own ATMs and instead contracted NCR Corp. to manufacture, distribute, and support them.[8]

Stan Welland, former head of Citibank's global technology infrastructure division, is credited with setting Citibank on its new outsourcing course.

"The times have changed," he said. "We're refocusing where we put our resources and what our core competencies are and, unlike the past, we're behaving as one bank, looking into what's proprietary and what we should buy, making maximum utilization of existing services and applications that are commercially available."

With Merrill Lynch, J.P. Morgan, Swiss Bank Corp., and many other financial institutions already doing the outsourcing dance, Citibank was a relative latecomer to the ball. Consequently, the temptation to jitterbug without warming up was intense.

Welland, though, surveyed his dance card and stayed cool. Such caution was wise, according to UBS Securities analyst Thomas H. Hanley, who wrote: "Success or failure from a competitive standpoint will largely depend on the effectiveness of investing prudently and executing properly in implementing technology decisions."

As for prudent investing, it was just as Rick had written on his notepad on that flight from California: "'Economy has frequently nothing to do with the money being spent, but with the wisdom used in spending it.' —Henry Ford."[9]

As for proper execution, Welland was keen to ensure that all outside technology providers work according to the same set of standards—on the network, the desktop, the LAN, and the entire infrastructure. "When you have control," he said; "you can communicate uniformly with suppliers, with members of your team, with customers—end users and internally at the bank." Without that control, he observed, "you just have anarchy—interface problems, severe downtime, and delays in building networks and delivering products on time."[10]

AT&T Solutions' Regional Managing Partner William Bangert reviewed Citibank's situation. As he recalls: "We began to realize that they were really serious. They had every conceivable legacy network technology, and it was obvious that something had to be done to rationalize the operation."

But who would Citibank choose to help them with this job?

Who could ensure the desired standards and control?

Who could provide cost-efficient, nonproprietary software applications for the specific business processes?

Who could manage the systems for data distribution, transaction processing, voice networking, and imaging services and thus liberate the bank to focus on banking instead of technological competencies—

and thereby become, in Welland's words, "the best banking enterprise in the world"?

The answer was soon to come:

INTER@CTIVE
WEEK

March 16, 1998

AT&T, CITIBANK SIGN HUGE CONTRACT

Citibank NA last week signed a five-year, $750 million deal with AT&T Corp. under which the communications giant will run Citibank's worldwide data network and lead the banking company's charge into electronic commerce.

The contract is the largest outsourcing deal signed in the financial services sector and also one of the biggest Internet-related services pacts to date. In addition, the deal represents a major breakthrough for AT&T's service unit, AT&T Solutions, which spent more than a year brokering the win.

"This agreement will serve as a milestone for enterprises to examine network outsourcing more seriously," said Gartner Group Inc. analyst Ken McGee.

Yankee Group analyst George Logemann agreed that the Citibank contract would dramatically raise industry confidence in network outsourcing and would inspire many more deals of this sort.

No doubt it would. Citibank's savings of $250 million over the life of the contract was the stuff of business dreams.

And belief and daring as well—to companies for which "Just Do It" was a call to glory, not just a marketing phrase.

In embracing network outsourcing in general and extolling AT&T Solutions' particular expertise, the home crowd was now cheering as one.

As more new contracts came in rapid succession, the partisans broke into a wave:

FOR RELEASE MONDAY, AUGUST 23, 1999
  AT&T WINS $400 MILLION CONTRACT
  FROM ALLIED SIGNAL

FOR RELEASE MONDAY, AUGUST 30, 1999
  STATE OF TEXAS NAMES AT&T
  TO SPEARHEAD TEX-AN 2000

FOR RELEASE TUESDAY, OCTOBER 29, 1999
  AT&T WINS CONTRACT FROM A. G. EDWARDS
  FOR NEW NETWORKING TECHNOLOGY

FOR RELEASE MONDAY, NOVEMBER 9, 1999
  AT&T WINS $125 MILLION CONTRACT
  FROM CVS FOR VOICE, DATA, AND
  MANAGED NETWORKING SERVICES

FOR RELEASE TUESDAY, NOVEMBER 30, 1999
  DELPHI AUTOMOTIVE SELECTS AT&T
  FOR GLOBAL NETWORKING

FOR RELEASE TUESDAY, NOVEMBER 30, 1999
  AT&T AWARDED CONTRACT FROM
  GENERAL MOTORS TO DESIGN, BUILD,
  AND MANAGE GLOBAL IP NETWORK

Rick explains part of what AT&T Solutions has done for GM:

They had a closed inventory system just for dealers, a legacy system, very clunky. It wasn't designed for the public to use. We said to them, "Why not open it to car buyers by making it Net-based? Let people shop for that purple Blazer anytime they want, not just during dealers' business hours. Let them see if it's somewhere in inventory or en route to a dealer or if it's even been manufactured yet."

GM now runs a TV commercial in which cars morph as a buyer walks through the lot. They change in size, color, and shape. The message is you can go online now and find any GM car you want, and you'll get it quickly. That's all thanks to our taking their legacy system and adapting it to the Net.

In recognition of AT&T Solutions' overall success, Rick was named the first corporate winner of the Outsourcing World Achievement Award in 1999.

Sponsored by PricewaterhouseCoopers and Michael F. Corbett & Associates, Ltd., the award honored Rick's and AT&T Solutions' achievements in making outsourcing a key management tool to increase companies' competitiveness and shareholder value.

Said Rick, "This award is affirmation of the ascendancy of networking in the outsourcing industry and especially of AT&T Solutions' growing leadership in this highly specialized segment of the market."

In the same year, the AT&T Solutions Web site, www.attsolutions. com, won the Gold Award at the San Francisco @d:tech trade show for online marketing and advertising. The award, for "Best Business-to-Business Commerce Web Site," was bestowed by a judging panel of 19 recognized leaders in the interactive marketing field.

In 1999 Rick also personally racked up an award of another sort: an appointment to the board of trustees of his alma mater, Stevens Institute of Technology.

"Mr. Roscitt brings very important perspective to the board," said Stevens President Harold J. Raveché, "including that of the rapid global growth of e-business and the strategic use of technology in competitive business practices."

Responded Rick, "I am particularly interested in using my experience in the business world to help shape a curriculum that will produce undergraduates who are just as proficient and conversant in management as they are in technology. There is a strong and growing need for graduates of this type."

Rick put his money behind his passionate words: A month after receiving his appointment he announced a $100,000 AT&T grant to Stevens Tech for the development of a new "E-Business" Bachelor of Science program blending practical application of science and technology with the study of core business functions such as production, marketing, supply-chain management, and customer service.

The innovative curriculum would examine how today's electronically bonded network of customers, suppliers, and creators of services and products affects business operations and tactical decision making.

Said Raveché, "Businesses today are starving for employees who are fluent in both the language of technology and the language of business. Through our newly developed "E-Business" B.S. programs, Stevens has not only crafted a university experience that offers students unparalleled options and greater earning power but also meets the needs of corporations for whom we have become an increasingly critical resource."

On the employment note, Rick revealed that AT&T would support the Stevens "e-degree" program by hosting a specific number of students through four-year work-study programs and would hire graduates of the program.

"These Stevens e-business graduates will be highly sought after," Rick said, "because they will not require the traditional time and training to become effective employees."

Remember Rick railing against static classrooms and chiding bookbound professors who plodded around their brick-and-mortar campuses—when their heads weren't stuck in the sand?

Raveché shared Rick's dismay. "Academia all too often stays true to its course and methodology in educating its students," he said. "At Stevens we have listened to the industry leaders and developed a program to address their concerns."

Not only was Stevens listening to industry leaders, it was hiring them to teach! Raveché's plan was to engage corporate "teaching executives" to instruct undergraduates in virtual networking, network applications, Web-enabled financial and consumer services, and technology management.

As we have heard Rick say, "Savvy, well-prepared human capital is very scarce."

More prone to acting than lamenting, Rick was partnering with academia to turn a scarcity into a rich supply.

This was fast-track education.

This was learning at the speed of light.

This was training at the speed of change.

With its well-stocked, heavy-hitting client roster and a basket of industry and academic accolades, AT&T Solutions was a certified home crowd favorite—a local hero without a doubt.

The measure of a truly great team, though, is not just claiming victory on home ground but also winning on the road.

DEBRIEFING

Nothing succeeds like success—but sometimes successful companies become *victims* of their own success and end up snatching defeat from the jaws of victory.

AT&T Solutions worried that in being so successful so early it might grow into a heavy, cautious corporate beast. After running at the speed of change, it might slow to a trot. As Rick said, "It's tough staying true to our founding vision while we're increasingly beholden to the corporation's shareholders."

Fortunately, AT&T Solutions was even more beholden to another stakeholder group: its customers. As we have attempted to make clear in this book, customer intimacy was an AT&T Solutions corporate value from the start. As we know from life, when two parties are intimate they have a tendency to reproduce. By staying bold, nimble, and sharp, AT&T Solutions tightened its bonds with existing customers and added many new ones to its Wall of Wins. In this way, the enterprise reproduced and multiplied its initial success.

Ask yourself the following questions. Each "yes" answer means that instead of just consolidating old business, you are boldly capitalizing on current success to cultivate new growth.

> Is your company multiplying its success? In the process, is it staying lean and hungry for more business? Is it adding muscle instead of just fat?
>
> Do you say "yes" to customers far more than you say "no"?
>
> Do you customize each customer solution instead of following a rule book or a set of precedents based on past success?
>
> Do you regularly refocus your corporate vision and reconfirm your values and culture?
>
> Are you staying down in the trenches with your customers instead of sitting high and dry and aloof?
>
> Do you see a competitor who is set aggressively to attack your turf? If so, do you have a business plan to meet the assault?
>
> Do you view your existing customer base as your best source of growth? Specifically, are you prepared to do the following?

- Cross-fertilize and enrich existing business.
- Seek ways to sow, cultivate, and harvest a bumper new business crop.
- Create competitive advantage by exploiting new technologies and managing costs.
- Become even more customer intimate with each account.

Chapter

10

Winning on the Road: We Are the World

$\mathbf{M}$ike Armstrong tells this story:

In the little village of Chandryel in rural Bangladesh, anyone who wanted to make a phone call used to have to travel eight kilometers to the closest regular pay phone.

Which often didn't work.

But then Delora Begum got a $350 development loan and invested it in a cellular phone, the first phone of any kind in the village.

Now the people of Chandryel come to Delora Begum's hut, and for a reasonable fee, they can use her phone to connect to the world.

Village farmers can call the capital to check on grain prices.

People who are ill can call for medical help.

And for the first time, a mother in Chandryel can talk to her emigrant son who drives a cab in New York.

This is all possible because a leading nonprofit institution in Bangladesh teamed up with the Norwegian phone company Telenor to build a rural wireless network that sells air time to people like Delora Begum, who has become known in the village as "the phone lady."[1]

Certainly, Bangladesh, like most developing nations, still has a long road to travel before creating a telecom infrastructure and a competitive market. But "the phone lady" represents one small pocket of progress, and a hope for a communications revolution in the less developed areas of the world.

For both the developed and the less developed world, the communications revolution presents enormous opportunities for enlightenment, joy, a higher standard of living, and longer life.

For providers of communications products and services, it opens huge markets, of course. One of Mike Armstrong's highest strategic priorities, therefore, is finding overseas clients and partners to support AT&T's relationships with multinational companies in the United States.

The number of people linked to the Internet worldwide has exploded from 10 million, less than four years ago, to around 200 million today, with 56 percent of users in the United States and Canada, 23 percent in Europe, and 17 percent in the Asia/Pacific region. It is predicted that there will be 1 billion users worldwide by 2010.

Correspondingly, e-commerce is no longer limited to the United States. As e-commerce explodes in Western Europe and industrialized Asia, our American share of this business is expected to decline to about 54 percent by 2003.

Will this mean the end of American e-commerce world leadership? Armstrong says it will not.

First, he asserts, the growth of e-commerce will continue to profit American firms that sell hardware and software around the world. In both products and intellectual capital, America will stay ahead.

Also, just as small, start-up Internet businesses have crashed the corporate giants' party in the United States, Armstrong sees no reason why they can't continue the party overseas.

Actually, he does see one reason for concern: high foreign phone rates keep Internet access charges intolerably high, and thus make Internet use unaffordable to all but the wealthy elite.

Without cheap and easy Internet access, the World Wide Web cannot be the free-to-all global forum it was envisioned to be, and it will become an exclusive, gated community instead.

In remarks released in March 2000 by the International Policy Institute, Armstrong stated, "For developing countries in particular, the basic building block of the Internet is easier and cheaper access to telecommunications. Without telecommunications, there is no Internet. The government is encouraging foreign countries to lower rates that U.S. carriers pay for telecommunications, and to lower domestic charges for Internet access. In too many countries, Internet access is kept artificially high by local phone rates. Just as in the United States, competition will bring local phone rates down. In contrast, it would retard the Internet's growth if the same market access restrictions telecom companies continue to face in many countries were simply transferred to the Internet. For countries to serve as gatekeepers to the Internet defies the very heart of the system—and its promise of freely available information."

Armstrong is pleased that the U.S. government is urging foreign countries to lower the rates that U.S. telecommunications carriers must pay. Ideally, foreign governments will not be Internet gatekeepers, but they will allow free competition to set phone rates at fair levels, and thus keep Web access charges in check.

Armstrong has also identified two other factors that are critical to ensuring American technological leadership in the future. "First," he states, "a strong and vibrant venture capital market, featuring low-cost access to capital, is an important factor in incubating new technologies and new companies to bring those technologies to market. We are the world leader in capital formation, and that must continue. Second, there is a worldwide shortage of qualified personnel to fill the jobs demanded by the new information economy. The United States should encourage the world's best software designers and other high-tech professionals to come here and work, for perhaps nowhere more than in technology industries, America is still the land of opportunity, where a rising tide lifts all boats."

The Internet's importance, however, is far greater than its ability to make private American companies rich.

"The Internet is transforming society around the world," Armstrong says. "It's taking the market system global. It reaches everyone.

It's worldwide, regardless of the system of government. The Internet freely conducts interactive communications, information exchange, and e-commerce, transparent to borders, bureaucracy, or belligerent governments. It frees people everywhere to see and hear the truth, to know reality, and to experience freedom of expression. Propaganda will no longer be able to perpetuate totalitarianism. And the Internet brings the efficiencies of a global market, direct distribution, and consumer choice to everyone—above and beyond the state of any nation's infrastructure and specific economy."

Opening and developing international markets is a high-priority goal for AT&T Solutions, as well.

Indeed, from the day it was born in 1995, AT&T Solutions had a global reach. In Europe, over 3000 AT&T personnel were immediately designated to provide AT&T Solutions' clients with a direct contact link. Seven new AT&T Network Solutions Centers were planned to provide European clients with a networking solutions "one-stop shop."

Pier Carlo Falotti, former president of AT&T Europe, said, "In Europe, we have a diverse range of customers with a diverse set of needs and requirements. They all have one thing in common: they know that information-intensive business, voice, data, video, and wireless networking can give them a strategic advantage in their own markets. They also know it is more efficient to choose a company with strong expertise in networking and computing to support their needs completely."

Sergio Giacoletto, former European president of AT&T Solutions, added, "By combining AT&T's established networking expertise in Europe, coupled with consultancy and systems integration, AT&T Solutions is well placed to offer customers exactly what they demand of us: complete end-to-end answers to their business problems. AT&T Solutions is tailored to a customer's exact needs."

AT&T Solutions isn't just in the United States and Europe, of course. Relationships with Chung-what Telecom in Taiwan, PT Telkom in Indonesia, the Ministry of Railways in China, and the Halla business group in Korea prove that.

Halla, a Korean heavy engineering industry pioneer, is a major Asian player in shipping, shipbuilding, automotive parts, industrial plants, construction, heavy construction equipment, cement, trade, resources development, communications, and newsprint. When it allied with

AT&T Solutions, it had 30 branch offices and affiliates in the United States, Canada, Europe, and throughout Asia/Pacific.

In this engagement, AT&T Solutions helped Halla Information Systems Corporation create an enterprisewide network to allow multimedia and video conferencing between Halla's 15 strategic business units and its headquarters in Seoul. Deployment was via an asynchronous transfer mode (ATM) network developed by AT&T Labs. The T1 (American standard) transmission circuit interconnected the switch nodes with each other, and the endpoints in Korea and in other countries. The result was high-speed video, data, and voice transmission to all the different sites.

"These new multimedia capabilities will help Halla companies improve our business productivity, making us more competitive in the global marketplace," said Jung-Sik Moon, president of Halla Information Systems Corporation. "We regard this enhancement to our information technology infrastructure as just the first step in fulfilling our vision to have the most efficient IT services to meet our needs, as well as our customers' future business requirements."

Ron Jenkins, AT&T Solutions' regional managing partner for Asia/Pacific Systems Integration Practice, had an equally sanguine view. "I am confident that this will be the first step in a long lasting relationship. We look forward to jointly developing market opportunities in the multimedia network services business."

Moon's and Jenkins' confidence was justified by subsequent events:

FOR RELEASE TUESDAY, MARCH 11, 1997

HALLA CHOOSES AT&T SOLUTIONS AGAIN

AT&T today announced that it has signed a US$3.75 million contract with the Mando Machinery Corporation, the flagship of the Halla business group. AT&T will provide consulting services to help Mando build a flexible, easily expandable infrastructure for information technology applications.

Mando Machinery Corporation, a leading producer of automotive components and systems, had been growing annually at an average rate of over 30 percent since its establishment in 1962. With 15 factories and over 8200 employees, it showed revenue of US$1.5 billion in 1996.

Under the 15-month contract, AT&T Solutions helped Mando deploy Oracle's Enterprise Resource Planning (ERP) software to facilitate planning, upgrade manufacturing control, and promote electronic commerce throughout the Halla business group—all toward saving resources, money, and time.

AT&T Solutions also provided professional assistance to help Mando examine and improve its current operational policies. In addition, it established ERP education and training programs for Mando's management and employees.

The undertaking was part of Mando's *Jung Bo Wha* project, designed to use the latest information technology to improve the company's business processes.

"This project has strategic significance, not only for Mando but also for the entire Halla business group," said Mando Machinery Corporation president Sang-Soo Oh. "Jung Bo Wha is our way of ensuring that Mando will continue to be competitive and remain an industry leader into the twenty-first century."[2]

AT&T bolstered its own twenty-first century global strategy in 1998 by acquiring IBM's Global Networking division—now called AT&T Global Network Services. The deal gives AT&T Solutions an international, multiprotocol network with 2000 dial-up points of presence linking more than 850 cities in 59 countries and handling the traffic of 1.2 million Internet users every day.

"My mother-in-law is 86," Mike Armstrong relates, "and a lot of life she sees through TV. So, when we acquired IBM's Global Network for some $5 billion, she called my wife and said, 'Isn't it wonderful after Mike spent all those years at IBM that he could buy it back.' And then she said, 'But don't you think $5 billion is a bit too much?'"[3]

It was a lot—but AT&T got more than just the IBM Global Network for its money. It also inherited IBM's close relationship with Japan's Nippon Telegraph & Telephone Corp. (NTT). Six months earlier, IBM and NTT had arranged for NTT's multinational business customers to use the IBM Network's high-speed connections to gain network access in 55 countries.

SCOTT PERRY'S STORY, PART 2: PARTNERING WITH NTT

The deal with NTT in Japan was a classic of cross-cultural complication. NTT is the world's biggest telecommunications services provider. AT&T

is second in revenue terms. NTT views us with great respect, and as their arch-competitor in many ways. And yet, over an 18-month period, we convinced them to invest in our AGNS-Japan business in their own country rather than inventing and developing a similar business themselves. At first, they claimed they already created a networking solutions business. But after we taught them what AGNS-Japan and AT&T Solutions were about, they acknowledged that we were far ahead of their business. So they decided to join our business instead of fighting with us.

The long process of negotiating was a really interesting and time-consuming project. Complicated by the language and cultural differences—both the way we talk about our business and the way we effectively work, as well as the way that executives interact with their people in accomplishing and creating a complicated alliance deal.

The net result is a most improbable one. NTT has invested in and become a partner in AT&T's Managed Solutions entities in Japan, AGNS-Japan, and with AT&T Solutions in their own country. And given the dramatic changes and the pace of continuing change in the networking solutions business, it is a completely sensible result.

Analysts saw how AT&T's global puzzle pieces were beginning to fit.

"Within a year," said Ken McGee of the Gartner Group, "you will see a more solid relationship between AT&T, British Telecommunications, and NTT."[4]

McGee was right.

As previously noted, AT&T had already launched a global joint venture with British Telecommunications—creating an enterprise called Concert to serve multinational business customers, international carriers, and Internet service providers. In the agreement, AT&T Solutions and British Telecom Syncordia Solutions (BTSS), BT's network outsourcing subsidiary, joined to provide managed data, voice, and video services in Europe, Asia, and Latin America. BTSS undertook to manage relationships with local phone companies overseas.

Said Armstrong, "With BT as our global partner, we'll be in a good position to deliver seamless global reach. The Global Venture will reach 237 countries. It will have 6000 private line nodes, 1000 frame relay nodes in more than 40 countries, and 200,000 international private line circuits."

A January 2000 contract with Acer, Inc., the world's third largest manufacturer of PCs, allowed AT&T Solutions, working with Concert, to extend its global, and specifically Asian reach.

In the seven-year, $100 million deal, AT&T Solutions and Concert are designing, building, and managing a state-of-the-art global IP network to transform Acer's six legacy networks into an integrated, global IP infrastructure. The resulting Acer Global Network, based on a scalable architecture, will provide advanced technology, reliable performance, and predictable costs. To manage the network, AT&T Solutions is establishing a global life-cycle management team in Taiwan.

By promoting collaboration between Acer's design and production facilities, and thus shortening product cycles—and by linking 56 sites in 37 countries, as well as supporting customers, dealers, and distributors in over 100 countries—the project aims to save the computer maker $15 million a year.

"Networking is a critical element for global enterprises," says Stan Shih, chairman and CEO of the Acer Group. "A smooth internal and external communications flow directly impacts a company's quality and efficiency. AT&T is a global leader in networking technology and management. I am confident that with AT&T's outstanding expertise we can significantly improve Acer's global logistics and service quality."

Adds Acer President Simon Lin, "Networking touches all aspects of business—global logistics, customer service, R&D, and e-commerce. AT&T's world-class networking capabilities will allow us to accelerate deployment of e-commerce applications and work more effectively with both customers and suppliers."

"The Acer Global Network will help propel Acer into the twenty-first century," states AT&T Solutions Asia/Pacific Managing Partner David Fu, "with Web-based, real-time electronic commerce applications a central element in its global business relationships."

AT&T Solutions was shocked by the demand for their services in Asia/Pacific. In fact, they have done almost as much networking integration overseas as they have done in the United States.

AT&T Solutions now spans the planet from New Jersey to Taiwan—with budding, developing, and flourishing engagements all in between.

In 1999 a poll conducted by The Yankee Group cited AT&T Solutions as the "best-positioned network outsourcer" in both the United States and Europe.

"We have to be global," Rick asserts. "If we're going to serve the 5000 largest corporations in the world, we have to go where they go. That doesn't necessarily mean we have to have a presence everywhere in the world. It does mean we'll be where a client needs us to be. Citi-corp, for example, is a global enterprise. They're in Latin America, they're in Europe, they're in Asia/Pacific, in a staggering total of 98 countries, and consequently, that's where we are."[5]

Working in foreign business environments presents unique chal-lenges—and not just for AT&T Solutions, of course.

Raymond E. Bayley is a partner and United States leader for busi-ness process outsourcing for PricewaterhouseCoopers.

"We're finding dramatic differences between North America, Asia, and Europe," he notes. "The kinds of things we're doing over there and the ways we create value wouldn't apply in a large, homogeneous mar-ket like the United States. Also, we find that, as much as we're knitting together forms around the world, when we get on the ground in South America, it's different from when we get on the ground in Warsaw or Denver. So we have to think differently about our outsourcing technol-ogy in each marketplace."

Russell Fradin is group president of employer services at ADP, Inc. in Roseland, New Jersey. In his experience, "Western Europe and Latin America are very similar to the United States, but Asia is the most resis-tant. We're having problems employing the same skill base in those economies that we employ here. We've looked at some potentially big partners over there, but we just haven't found the right fit yet."

Rick inserts, "It's tough to work in Japan because of culture, and in Germany because of their strong labor laws. Nevertheless, two of our biggest engagements have been in Germany and Japan."

Despite his own company's frustrations in Asia, Russell Fradin fore-sees a global outsourcing boom. "The idea that we're going to keep outsourcing a secret here in North America is absurd."

James Brian Quinn, professor emeritus at the Amos Tuck School of Business at Dartmouth College, thinks the boom isn't booming fast enough.

"What I see happening abroad is that the big companies have been slow," he says, adding that as economies of scale have gone away, scale has restricted speed.

The federal government should do more to encourage outsourcing, Quinn believes. "Part of our problem is to get the bureaucrats in Wash-ington to understand that they're dealing with a model that was designed back in the late 1800s, partially by Karl Marx."[6]

AT&T Solutions, Quinn would admit, has not been slow in pursuing global outsourcing. The AT&T Solutions Global Client Support Centers can claim large credit for that efficiency and speed.

Domestically based in North Carolina and Ohio, and with operations centers in Britain, the Netherlands, India, and Singapore, the GCSCs keep clients connected to their own clients, customers, suppliers, and employees, virtually anywhere in the world.

An AT&T Solutions trade advertisement declares:

**MILLIONS OF CUSTOMERS,
BILLIONS OF TRANSACTIONS,
TRILLIONS OF DOLLARS.
ONE GLOBAL NETWORKING COMPANY.**

A multibillion-dollar transaction can occur between any two points on the globe in less time than it takes you to read this sentence.

Or not.[7]

"To be or not to be," as Hamlet said.

AT&T Solutions eliminates the "not."

By helping companies take arms against the slings and arrows of outrageous fortune, AT&T Solutions empowers them to make outrageous fortunes of their own.

To sleep—perchance to dream...to believe...to dare...to do...

DEBRIEFING

Customer intimacy exists when a company's bond with its customers is extraordinarily close. After becoming intimate with many domestic customers, AT&T Solutions proved that it could do the same with customers located an ocean or more away.

You can, too.

Beware, though: The death of distance in the physical sense does not immediately guarantee the crystal clear, light-speed interchange that this era promises more temptingly every day. You must do more than just talk with your customers. You must communicate with them head-to-head and heart-to-heart. This is more challenging in the international realm, of course, where linguistic and cultural differences can send the most directly aimed signal astray.

For example, imagine yourself greeting your foreign counterpart with a handshake while he is welcoming you instead with a bow. Is this a promising start to your relationship?

You then begin talking to each other from three feet apart but in your respective native languages. Do you wonder why neither of you is getting through?

Clearly, becoming intimate with foreign customers requires you to acculturate not just within your own company, but in a global sense, as well.

We've likened customer intimacy to a tango. In the new global economy, you and your international customers must become mutually responsive dance partners—instead of soloists taking star turns.

Here's how to take your first steps:

- Decide if doing business with foreign customers is a strategic priority for your company.
- Determine if your Internet strategy is global in scope.
- Acknowledge, study, and accommodate the distinct languages and cultures of your foreign customers.
- Decide whether you will be a stay-at-home global player, or one with physical presences abroad.
- Distinguish the ways to create value in diverse foreign markets from the ways you create value in the large, homogeneous market of the United States.
- Select the appropriate skill base to use in each foreign market (as distinct from the skill base you use here at home).
- Recruit and hire sufficient personnel to fill the jobs being created in the new global economy.
- Discuss the dreams as well as the goals of your foreign customers.

Chapter

11

Winning in Your Own Company: Let the Games Begin

In a June 2000 speech to the New York Association for Business Economics, Federal Reserve Chairman Alan Greenspan reflected on the last five years of the twentieth century.

"What differentiates this period from other periods in history," he said, "is the extraordinary role played by information and communication technologies. The effect of these technologies could rival and arguably surpass the impact the telegraph had prior to the Civil War."[1]

Ignited by high-tech, dotcom companies, the communications revolution is spurring old-line brick-and-mortar manufacturing firms to rethink, redesign, and reengineer their design processes, factory floors, supply chains, and distribution channels.

For example, to streamline manufacturing processes and save costs, Ford has joined with GM and DaimlerChrysler to create Covisint, the largest business-to-business exchange on the planet. Through Covisint

—which stands for Collaboration, Vision, and Integrity—each company posts its car component needs to 50,000 suppliers around the world, who then bid for the orders.

In the "old economy," Ford's average purchase order transaction cost was $150. With the real-time Covisint system, it's $15. Clearly, cost-efficient Internet-based networking is replacing traditional economies of scale.

"This is absolutely a transformation of Ford," says Ford's President of Internet Strategy Brian Kelly. "Ultimately this is about the redistribution of assets, capital, and competitive advantage."

By enabling manufacturers of all kinds to determine customer needs before fabricating products, the Internet permits companies to "pull" the products through the supply chain in accordance with customer demand, instead of "pushing" them through, based on marketplace presumptions and hopes fueled by advertising.

"We want to use the Internet to build cars that people want and not build inventory," states Jeff Dossett, president of CarPoint, an alliance between his own company, Microsoft, and Ford.

"Consumers want to feel they are in control of the buying process," adds Mark Roman, Ford's liaison with the Microsoft alliance.[2]

While responding more sensitively and efficiently to customer demand, Ford is taking a visionary approach to product supply. It recently introduced the Escape, an SUV that burns 25 percent less fuel than other vehicles in its class, and can save its owners $2400 during its useful life.

The reduced fuel consumption will benefit the atmosphere, too, of course.

But is saving customers money or saving the planet Ford's main concern?

Both are, explains Jacques Nasser, Ford's CEO: "There is a growing connection between the community, social needs, the economy, business, everything that we do, and it's really being driven by the Internet, e-commerce, and the breaking down of trade barriers and capital market barriers. And people really do expect that corporations such as the Ford Motor Company have high values and a corporate philosophy that takes all of this into account."

Ford is spreading the Internet-age wealth to its own employees as well, providing free computers and printers to its 335,000-member global workforce. Says Nasser, "The whole idea here is to take this new technology, this Internet, and allow our workforce to develop their optimal level of intellectual capability, . . . to become more productive, and to be more connected to the marketplace."

In the next decade, Ford and other large companies such as GM and GE will focus less on selling products and more on solving customer problems, and will form alliances with key partners as a result. In so doing, they will be acting less like "old economy" manufacturers and more like such new-economy leaders as Cisco and Dell.

Their corporate cultures will sharpen and quicken.

They will be reborn, and thus they will truly mature.

"Big companies like us were frightened by the Net," admits GE's former chairman Jack Welch. "We thought the creation of Web operations was mysterious Nobel Prize stuff, the province of the wild-eyed and purple-haired. As we have gotten more deeply into it, we have learned that digitizing is the easiest part. E-business was made for GE. The "E" in GE now has a whole new meaning."

Welch announced to shareholders that e-business would "change the DNA of GE forever." He put the sales and marketing teams on red alert. "One cannot be tentative about this," he declared. "Delay brings the risk of being cut out of your own market, perhaps not by the traditional competitors but by companies you never heard of 24 months ago." Just as networking is changing the way blue-chip manufacturing companies do business in the twenty-first century, so it is changing companies of all sizes in all industries.

If it hasn't already changed your company, it can.

It must.

And—if you adopt AT&T Solutions' guiding principles—it will.

Dream. Believe. Dare. Do.

All verbs, you notice, not static nouns—and all energized by the following value-creating ideals and their supporting actions (see Exhibit 9).

Vision

Dream beyond today's business.
Create a shared corporate story.
Develop plans to implement the vision to overcome barriers.

Values

Identify core values to help guide decision making.

Cascade values throughout the organization.

Establish synergy between employees and customers.

Alliances

Invest in brainware; outsource nonessentials.

Create long-lasting partnerships.

Don't play the blame game with partners.

Treat each alliance partner as a unique individual.

Acculturation

Establish a culture of collective commitment involving all employees at every level.

Lead your teams to execute the Dream, Believe, Dare, Do principles.

Reduce your policy manual by 50 percent.

Customer Intimacy

Define customer problems and dreams.

Create solutions that add value.

Fire impossible customers.

Create customers for life.

Measure, measure, measure.

Predictable Problems/Failing Forward Fast

Identify potential barriers to success.

Remove barriers that inhibit growth.

Develop processes or guidelines.

Celebrate failure and learn from it.

Quintessential Teams

Encourage and enable team members to continuously reinvent themselves and their work.

Establish project- or process-focused QTs.

Co-locate to be customer-intimate.

Create a schedule cop.

Give QTs their own place to work.

Create fun.

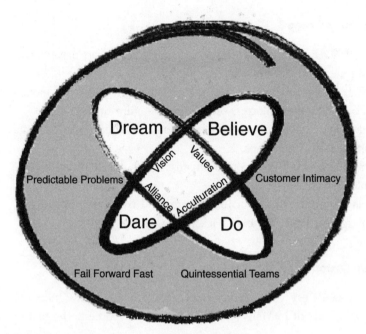

Exhibit 9 Leading at the Speed of Change Model

CAUTIONS

Start-up companies take off like firecrackers, whistling into the night sky, then bursting into dazzling arcs.

And then some of them, like firecrackers, fizzle and smoke and drift back down to earth.

Is your company a firecracker? Would you like it to be—at least through the dazzling arcs?

How can you avoid the fizzle and smoke?

For starters, don't be a firecracker; be a high-revving engine instead—because engines can be refueled and retuned to keep from chugging to a halt.

AT&T Solutions is a high-revving engine, unique in that it was lifted from the 120-year-old chassis of AT&T. Self-powered now for five years, AT&T Solutions occasionally sputters and slows down, but always gears back up.

How can you keep your own enterprise's engine revving at high RPMs?

Check for the following signs of corrosion and wear.

Bureaucracy Creep

In their early days, start-up entrepreneurs are like go-kart drivers, racing by the seat of their pants.

In their early maturity, they're in stock cars, with dashboard gauges and radio links to their spotters on the grandstand roof.

At the first signs of gray, they experience handling problems and make pit stops every few laps.

Certainly, it's foolish to drive an unsafe car, but a little shimmy shouldn't keep you off the track.

Pay attention to what your instruments and your pit crew tell you, but don't ignore what your own backside has to say.

Attitude Droop

In start-up mode everyone works insanely long hours. It's the Indy 500 and the 24 Hours of LeMans all in one—with adrenaline as the fuel in the tank.

Then some people burn out and pull off onto the breakdown lane, or just quit.

Others lose energy with the rise of an enervating "business-as-usual" sense.

Here are ways to restart these people's motors and keep their revs up:

- Rotate assignments
- Vary procedures
- Give a standing ovation to the top team-centric performer of the month
- Recognize positive behavior as well as good business results
- Have fun and celebrate success (see "Find New Ways to Have Fun" at the end of Chapter 7)

Communication Lag

Back in that "broom closet," AT&T Solutions' original band of 12 could address each other face-to-face. Ideas floated on Monday were policy by Wednesday night.

With expansion, AT&T Solutions people gathered together in "town meetings."

Now, with 10,000 employees in 60 countries, it's impossible for everyone to physically gather in one place. Thus it takes longer for ideas to be discussed, debated, reviewed, approved by all concerned personnel, and put into operational shape.

It need not take forever, though. A total communication breakdown doesn't have to be the price of burgeoning success.

You can do as AT&T and AT&T Solutions have done: come together virtually instead of massing in a physical site.

Speed Limits

Driving at 55 miles per hour saves lives on the highway.

In business it's sure death.

Too often we mistake targets for limits.

Hey, we improved deal completion cycle time from 100 days to 50 days—wonderful!

Now let's get it down to 10 days.

12

United We Stand, Divided We Stand

*P**lus ça change, plus c'est la meme chose*—the more things change, the more they stay the same.

This old adage has elements of both truth and fallacy.

It's true in that the Internet has not changed the law of business evolution: the fittest still survive.

It's not true in that the *means* of survival have been transformed to a stunning degree.

AT&T Solutions seized those means, not just to survive but to thrive.

As AT&T chairman and CEO, Mike Armstrong pursued an equally aggressive course, acquiring diverse outside resources to transform the voice long-distance carrier into a diversified communications powerhouse.

Here is a review of Armstrong's key expansionist initiatives:

- In 1998 he launched a global joint venture with British Telecommunications PLC, creating the enterprise called Concert to serve multinational business customers, international carriers, and Internet service providers.

- Also in 1998, he purchased Teleport Communications Group, Vanguard Cellular Systems, Inc., and Tele-Communications, Inc.[1]
- In 2000 he acquired MediaOne Group, thus completing the establishment of the nation's largest cable network.

Tele-Communications and MediaOne had been two of the largest cable systems in America, and their acquisition cost Armstrong over $100 billion of AT&T's stock value. Wall Street, though, cheered the new aggressive strategy and sent AT&T's share price—which had been at a six-year low when Armstrong arrived—to record highs. Analysts and investors embraced Armstrong's vision of transforming AT&T from a voice long-distance company to a leader in wireless, data, and broadband services.

Internally, Armstrong decided in 1999 to consolidate AT&T's corporate communications service units—including AT&T Solutions—into a single division called AT&T Business Services (ABS). Also part of ABS would be AT&T Data and Internet Services and AT&T Global Network Services. The AT&T global sales organization would provide worldwide marketing support.

In December 1999 Rick was named president of ABS. Rick's charge was managing ABS's brand marketing, overseeing product and service development, and coordinating delivery and sales domestically and abroad.

In July 2000, *USA Today* observed: "The transformation Armstrong is attempting is one of the most sweeping and difficult in the history of American business. He is trying to reshape a venerable former monopoly dependent on a declining business into an Internet-age competitor with a hand in nearly all the industry's growth businesses."

Armstrong knew the sweep of his adventure and understood its difficulty. For a start, the networks had to be transformed to digital, on-net services had to be bundled, and the businesses had to be scaled. After two years, the wireless, cable, and data services units were beginning to scale, but the decline in long-distance was accelerating.

Also, some investors grew impatient with the slow but steady pace of upgrading the cable system, while the acquisition of MediaOne took longer than expected.

Worse yet, the unexpectedly rapid fall of long-distance prices due to discount competition undermined AT&T's revenue projections. Though long-distance had been faltering when Armstrong arrived in 1997, it still contributed 82 percent of total corporate revenue in January 1998 and was counted on to sustain the corporation during the transition to a bundled services strategy. However, intensifying competition from WorldCom, Sprint, the Baby Bells, wireless, and e-mail began draining profit from long-distance at a faster-than-expected rate and put the cash cow at risk of drying up.

"[AT&T] paid a lot in acquisition costs for the cable franchises," says David Eidelman, a money manager at Eidelman, Finger & Harris in Clayton, Missouri. "They thought they'd have the cash flow from long-distance to pay off that debt." Unfortunately, long-distance revenues proved "neither durable nor sustainable," in Mike Armstrong's own words.

As a result of these combined troubles, AT&T's overall operations were growing more slowly and earning less by mid-2000 than the company had led the market to expect. Most surprising—and painful—was the underachievement of the supposedly stalwart Business Services division, whose sales force had literally lost track of several big corporate customers when they were being shifted to AT&T's international Concert co-venture. This lapse allowed such competitors as World-Com and Sprint to step in and sell new data services to these accounts. By mid-2000, the AT&T Business Services unit was falling short of its predicted 9 to 11 percent growth rate—growing at 8 percent instead.

"The relationships, the administrative support, the skill coverage in those accounts was not carefully managed," Mike Armstrong admitted at a later date. On May 1, 2000, he faced making a confession of a larger sort:

The New York Times

SUNDAY, JULY 9, 2000

WITH AT&T AT THE BRINK, PRESSURES RISE AT THE TOP

It was the evening of Monday, May 1, and C. Michael Armstrong, the chairman of AT&T, needed help.

Huddled in a conference room at the company's headquarters in Basking Ridge, New Jersey, with key members of his executive team, Mr. Armstrong said he turned for advice to two Wall Street analysts, later identified by people close to the meeting as Frank J. Governali of Goldman, Sachs, and Jack Grubman of Salomon Smith Barney. Mr. Armstrong asked the two just how he should tell investors that some of AT&T's core businesses had stumbled. At least as important, Mr. Armstrong also wanted their assessment of how AT&T's shares, one of the nation's most widely held stocks, would react to the bad news.

"The analysts came in and they said, 'Well, look, what you have to do is just put this on the table, tell it like you're going to tell it,'" Mr. Armstrong recounted in an interview late last month. "'You're being forthright, you're talking about something in the future.' . . . Their bottom line was, 'You'll probably take a four to seven point hit and then bounce back, for a three to five point problem.' That's what their judgment was to me."

As it turned out, the analysts' judgment was well off the mark. After Armstrong made his announcement the next morning, AT&T's shares slid $7.9625 from the previous day's close of $49, thus slicing over $25 billion from AT&T's market value. (Shares had traded at $60 in mid-March.) In the following days the stock continued to fall instead of bounce back. In early July the stock price stood at $33.25. In the third quarter of 2000, as long-distance was accounting for 60 to 65 percent of AT&T's overall revenues, the company's profits fell 19.4 percent from the previous year, to $1.3 billion. It was true that the rest of AT&T grew at a 12 percent rate in the first quarter of 2000 and at 20 percent over the year's first nine months. However, the lagging long-distance revenues dragged the overall corporate growth down to 5 percent. By the end of October 2000, AT&T stock stood at around $22, about where it had been when Armstrong became CEO.

"The Street has gotten very emotional about this stock," said Daniel P. Reingold, chief telecommunications analyst for Credit Suisse First Boston. "It seems that every fear in the world has found its way into this stock and it has led to a very oversold condition. It's going to take good news on revenue or structural shock treatment, like some spin-offs or additional tracking stocks, to unlock the hidden value. But patient investors should be rewarded very handsomely."

As *The New York Times* reported, "It is not just AT&T's shares that are feeling the burn. For the first time since he took over as chairman and CEO in the fall of 1997, Mr. Armstrong himself is on the defensive. His bet-the-company vision to transform AT&T by delivering a package of interactive digital television, high-speed cyberspace access, and local telephone service over cable television lines is still largely just that, a vision."

Armstrong's vision, though, still burned bright. "I think that we're making progress," he said. "I think a lot of the progress is masked by financials as a result of the declining voice business. . . . What gives me confidence . . . is that the investments and the strategy are working. I see it, and the people who take the time to look at our company know it."

Too many shareholders did not see or know it, though—and their patience for profitable results was wearing thin. They weren't impressed by declarations that AT&T—if the long-distance unit were set apart—grew at 12 to 20 percent during 2000. They weren't impressed because the long-distance unit was *not* set apart—it was very much attached, like a cancer on the corporate body. As such, it needed to be cured or lanced. Though obstinately optimistic about AT&T overall, Armstrong was not blind to the grim fact that no cure for the ailing long-distance business was in sight. And so he pragmatically contemplated cutting it off.

"A business has to reach three conditions and then I would consider a segmentation of it," Armstrong said. "Is it operationally prepared for public investment? Will it create a currency that would serve a purpose? And will there be some value creation as a result of doing it?"

He answered his own questions as follows:

"Well, [the long-distance operation is] 115 years old, so I think it . . . operationally knows what it's doing. The creation of the currency is more obscure, because it has declining revenue. On the other hand, the currency would obviously have a value greater than it now has. And then the third, would it create shareholder value? In this case, it would permit that if there was some segmentation for the rest of AT&T."

Some segmentation for the rest of AT&T. Did this mean a breakup of the whole company? If so, it wouldn't be the first time that AT&T split itself up. In 1984 a federal antitrust ruling forced it to spin off its local phone operations, which became the Baby Bells. In 1996 AT&T voluntarily spun off its telecommunications equipment division as Lucent Technologies, Inc., and its computer division as NCR Corp.

Armstrong's mantra for an agglomerated AT&T was, in effect, "United We Stand." Now, as he considered surgery to restore the company's financial and operational health, he was about to make "Divided We Stand" the new rallying cry.

NO. 1 IN THE USA

THURSDAY, OCTOBER 26, 2000

IT'S OFFICIAL: AT&T PLANS 4-WAY SPLIT TO REVIVE STOCK

AT&T said Wednesday that it will split into four companies in its biggest overhaul since 1984's court-ordered breakup that spawned the regional Bells.

The expected move marks a dramatic effort to resuscitate a stock down nearly 50% this year as long-distance prices have fallen. It also signals at least a partial retreat from AT&T's bid to offer one-stop shopping for local, long-distance, and wireless phone services, cable TV, and high-speed Internet access.

"Project Grand Slam," as the breakup plan is called, is now underway and will divide AT&T as follows:

Business Services. This already existing 18,000-employee unit will provide voice, data, and networking services to corporate customers. In doing so, it will be able to cross-sell services from the other three units. Primary competitors will be Sprint and World-Com.

Consumer Services. With 18,000 employees, the long-distance residential phone service and WorldNet Internet service will be a subsidiary of Business Services. By 2002, its revenues are expected to be 35 percent of the four new companies' total. Consumer Services will trade as a tracking stock, to be issued in 2001. Customers have been assured of minimal change in their service. Primary competitors will be Sprint, WorldCom, and the Baby Bells.

Wireless. The 18,000-employee wireless phone unit—currently trading as a tracking stock with 15 percent publicly held—will be converted into an independent public company by summer 2001. It will market cell phones and mobile phone service to consumer and business accounts. Significant competitors will be Sprint, PCS, Verizon Wireless, and VoiceStream.

Broadband. The cable, TV, phone, and high-speed Internet unit will become a freestanding company, first as a tracking stock in 2001 and then as a common stock by 2002. With 37,000 employees, it is already the nation's largest cable operator. Its strongest competitors will be AOL–Time Warner, Cablevision, and Charter Communications.

Though distinct and freestanding, the four units will remain under the AT&T corporate umbrella—but in a brand-name more than an operational sense. Liberated to set their own goals and devise their own strategies, the units will grow and become profitable more quickly than they would under corporate control—or so Armstrong predicts. "With their resources and asset-based stock they can shape their own destiny and future," he proclaims. His presumption is that investors will begin valuing the robust wireless and broadband units on their own merits and will stop obsessing over the dwindling long-distance business. The combined stock price of all the units should thus be enhanced.

Employees will be "more highly motivated," insists Armstrong, and "shareowners should get the full value of their investment." His own aunt's healthy dividend checks will continue arriving, he says, so she'll lose no sleep over the company's transformation.

Wall Street wasn't counting on such peaceful nights, though—especially with AT&T admitting that the next combined dividend paid by the four stocks would likely be "substantially less" than the October 2000 payment of 88 cents per share. On the day of the breakup announcement, AT&T stock dropped 13 percent, losing $3.50 to close at $23.38—its lowest level in 10 years. It slipped 5.5 percent more by the end of that week.

"They are making operations more difficult by throwing everyone into chaos again," said Janney Montgomery Scott analyst Anna-Maria Kovacs as she downgraded AT&T stock to "sell." "When you have a company under pretty severe attack from the outside and you exacerbate that with a disorienting reorganization, I don't get very optimistic," she explained.

David Lefkowitz, an analyst at Credit Suisse Asset Management, said AT&T shares are "probably dead money for some time." Salomon Smith Barney analyst Jack Grubman downgraded the stock for the second time in two weeks and described it as "melting down."

In dividing the company, Armstrong had assumed that overall shareholder value would grow as the stock price of the individual units increased—even as long-distance declined. In other words, the sum of the freestanding parts would be worth more than the former consolidated whole.

Paul Krugman, writing in *The New York Times*, felt that this would be true only if AT&T were extremely undervalued today, if the new independent units were highly overvalued, or if both unlikely situations turned out to exist.

Some of the very brokerage firms reaping huge fees to split up AT&T were similarly pessimistic about Project Grand Slam's success. One by one they downgraded AT&T stock even as they were spinning off units to ostensibly prop it up.

In *The New York Times*, Gretchen Morgenson stated that Mike Armstrong shouldn't be surprised by these brokerage firms playing both sides of the fence. She also noted that the rosy financial promises of Armstrong's initial mergers had depended on rising stock prices and continuing ready access to capital. When the stock price plummeted and the capital slipped away, so did the prospects of success. Despite vowing to pay down much of its short-term debt with proceeds from the breakup, AT&T was likely to remain heavily leveraged for some time.

Added to AT&T's burden of debt was the residual weight of its old-economy structure and operational mechanisms. "The four new entities will likely perform as poorly as they do now," said Gartner Group analyst Ken McGee. "The same problems—a less than lean workforce, slowness to market, and ponderous bureaucracy—likely will plague each company."

Not all reaction to the breakup was negative, though. "The real bread and butter for corporations is data," said Ed Minyard, executive vice president and COO of New York–based StrategiNet, an AT&T data service customer. "I'd rather see [research and development] dollars go to the evolution of advanced services, rather than have the company continue to be dragged down trying to keep up with the Joneses in consumer long-distance."

Analyst Jeffrey Kagan, though, wondered if the split-up weakened AT&T's competitive position in the telecom industry. "The whole idea lately is to put a seamless front on services," Kagan said. "There is no way this is going to be a plus for them competitively. It's really just for stock prices."

But was it really just for stock prices? Was Wall Street now calling AT&T's operational shots?

"The balance has clearly swung in favor of shareholders," said Michael Jones, CTO of Flashcom, a Huntington Beach, California–based Internet service provider and AT&T customer.

Mike Armstrong disagreed. "I hope to dispel the myth that it's for any short-term purpose or for any lack of operational execution as some like to suggest," he declared. "Fundamentally, it's not only the next logical step but the next necessary step in the transformation of this company. The strategy for customers and shareholders has been consistent. Today we have decided to use the [company's] structure to best serve that strategy."

Armstrong was saying that only *structure* had changed, not strategy. Splitting up AT&T was not counter to bulking the company up; it was a natural outgrowth of bulking up. The one-stop shop was now merely inviting customers in through four doors instead of just one.

Salomon Smith Barney's Jack Grubman, though, didn't see the breakup in such natural evolutionary terms. "AT&T made a big deal about creating an integrated communications company selling bundled services," he said. "That is being abandoned after less than two years of trying."

New York magazine was more blunt in declaring Mike Armstrong's vertical ascent a total flop.

"The strategy was not given ample time to work," Jack Grubman remarked, implying that with more time it *might* have worked. Armstrong didn't have more time, though, as the pressures to appease skittish investors and gloomy analysts finally became too strong to resist.

Paul Krugman had been skeptical that a divided AT&T would be more valuable than the former united corporation, but he acknowledged the potential synergistic benefits of related businesses being gathered under one corporate roof. The risk, though, was a loss of corporate focus—and thus, we would add, of efficiencies and economies, too.

Risk, though, comes with a CEO's territory, as Mike Armstrong well knew. "This is the toughest of times, when people view their success in terms of the stock price," he said. "Transformation doesn't come easy. It comes from hard work and ramping up new products and services with new people and new technology, and we're doing that. I don't mind if people wonder if it can be done, this transformation. But I do mind if people wonder if it can be done when it's being done. And it's being done here."

Dream, Believe, Dare, *DO.*

Armstrong was a doer, no doubt about that. In the early 1980s he had steered the introduction of the IBM personal computer while market "experts" were predicting that individuals would never put a 16-bit machine on their desks. As chairman and CEO of Hughes Electronics Corporation in 1992, he had offset the post–Cold War loss of military contracts by investing in new civilian satellite systems.

Splitting up AT&T gained him more critical attention, though, than any of his previous endeavors. "This is more visible," he said. "I've never enjoyed so many critics and authors and helpers from the outside [telling me] what I should have done and what I could do."

Those critics and authors and helpers had the benefit of hindsight, of course, whereas Armstrong had had to peer around the 8-ball to see the road ahead. As critics, authors, and helpers ourselves, we need to consider what Armstrong could have and perhaps should have done along the way, while giving him credit for actions that were visionary, wise, and bold. When your strategy succeeds, you are "persistent and focused." But when it fails, you are "immovable and narrow-minded."

While external factors hampered Mike Armstrong's efforts to remake AT&T into a megapurveyor of bundled services, internal stresses caused by his large-scale reorganization, cost-cutting, and layoffs hurt, too. In trying to strengthen and invigorate a hidebound corporation, Armstrong inevitably destabilized it to a certain degree. A strong, unified company can survive destabilization and even come out stronger and more unified than before. AT&T, though, was in transition between its tradition-bound, bureaucratic past and its nimbler, more adventurous, AT&T Solutions–inspired future. In this position, its strength and unity were tentative at best. To successfully transform itself—first by expanding and agglomerating, and second by splitting up—AT&T needed maximum nurturing and minimum shock. Before *Daring* to grow at a dotcom pace and *Doing* massive deals to gain colossal strength, the company needed to reaffirm, communicate, and collectively acknowledge its new *Dreams* and *Belief* and support them by acting in accordance with the ideals espoused in this book.

VISION

Armstrong's initial vision was as wide as it was deep. In projecting AT&T as a massive emporium of bundled, on-net communications services, he nobly and bravely strategized to engorge the flagging company with new lifeblood. Accordingly, he focused collective attention and energy on creating a global business empire upon which the sun would never set.

Armstrong's vision, though, was not sharp enough to see how difficult empire building might be and thus how long it might take. He could not foresee the speed with which technology and regulation would transform the industry. Nor could he have predicted the market's reaction.

VALUES

Armstrong performed beautifully on May 2, 2000, when he told investors that underperformance by certain AT&T divisions was eroding the overall rate of corporate growth. While it was no secret that long-distance revenues had dropped, Armstrong could have put off a formal announcement or given it some sort of artificially positive spin. To his credit, he did not.

"I don't think withholding information is a good idea," he remarked. At a moment when the truth exposed him to a substantial financial hit, he proved that he meant what he said. However, when the hit was harder than he expected, his doggedly upbeat attitude seemed forced. When the company was eventually split up—sending shock waves through AT&T and Wall Street alike—he cheerfully wrote to employees, "The changes for most of you on a day-to-day basis will be small. The big change is in the exciting opportunity we gain by multiplying AT&T by the power of four." The message sounded more like public relations prose than heart-to-heart straight talk. In trivializing the disorienting effects of corporate upheaval and essentially dismissing employees' personal anxieties, Armstrong was pumping business results at the expense of the human element that would produce them. Therefore, the value of his truth—and thus his personal credibility—was diminished.

CUSTOMER INTIMACY

AT&T Solutions President Brian Maloney says this about Mike Armstrong: "I call him and say I need help with a CEO of another firm: let's go close some business. And he's right there; he's with me every step of the way. He brings such talent to the table. He engenders such respect with CEOs, they love him."

Mike Armstrong does not keep corporate customers at arm's reach. His arm is always fully extended, ready to shake hands in greeting and in closing a deal. He senses corporate customers' needs, he believes, because his finger is on their pulse. When he was acquiring companies to create a communications monolith, he said this: "To offer the kind of value our customers want we have to be facilities-based. This means offering a seamless set of on-net services, functions, features, performance, reliability, and cost that extend around the world and support our customers as they take their business to their own customers."

He felt he knew residential customers, too, and believed market research that said they would want to buy a full array of long-distance, wireless, and broadband cable services from one source.

No wonder he was surprised when only 10 percent of current AT&T customers actually signed up. Their indifference was a bitter pill that forced Armstrong to admit: "Customers would rather see an automotive lube job coupled with their long-distance carrier than wireless phones and TV."

Why didn't market research reveal that customers might be indifferent to a communications services one-stop shop?

Didn't we say in this book that market research was an old-line activity that zeroed in on customers more as targets than as prequalified and eager consumers of services and goods?

And weren't we specific in criticizing research that led to developing production-line offerings in a ready-aim-fire marketing approach?

That's what AT&T's initial research amounted to. And while its real-life experience demonstrated that there is a large and strong market for "natural" bundles, such as local and long-distance, it also showed that consumers are perfectly willing to take cable TV from Cablevision and wireless service from Verizon while phoning long-distance via WorldCom or Sprint.

In fact, we champion market research that is probing, wide-ranging, and capable of leading to customized instead of generic marketing. This doesn't rule out occasional leaps of faith—as long as the faith is grounded on knowledge gained in the street. Before launching AT&T Solutions, the team of 12 learned all they could about what potential customers and suppliers might want. Before that, they had listened to a customer—Chase Manhattan Bank—who had expressed a crying need for network services and had urged AT&T to be its outsourcer of choice. At that point AT&T Solutions was an idea whose time had come. The idea came from the clients who inspired them at every turn.

Was the vision of a bundled services conglomerate an idea whose time had come? After two years, customers and investors said no. But would they have changed their minds if the strategy had been given more time to work? We'll never know the answer to that question, and in this sense the issue is moot. However, given the well-known impatience of investors and the preexisting unreceptivity of consumers to bundled services, it must be asked if the project should ever have been launched.

ACCULTURATION

As the first outsider to lead AT&T in its 120-year history, Mike Armstrong was just what the sclerotic company felt it needed at the top: new blood. "There was tremendous pressure to lead, with an exclamation point," says Jim Collins, author of the best-seller *Built to Last.*

Armstrong led from day one, cutting costs, reorganizing, laying off personnel, and buying communications companies in a $100 billion spending spree. These actions were shocks to AT&T culture, which was still suffering post-traumatic stress after the federally mandated divestitures of 1984. Since that time, AT&T CEOs Jim Olson and Robert Allen had taken structural and organizational initiatives but had done little to address cultural concerns about AT&T's core identity.

Was AT&T a phone company or a communications emporium? Did it favor residential consumers over corporate customers, or the other way around? Should the company project an image of rock-solid reliability or high-flying acquisitional zeal? Should it honor long-time shareholders by protecting its stock price, or dazzle the market by spiking shares to new heights?

These were business questions, of course, but since business is conducted by living, breathing, thinking, and feeling people, they needed to be addressed from a cultural point of view. As an outsider, Armstrong was at a disadvantage in doing this because he lacked an innate understanding of AT&T culture. It wasn't in his blood. Consequently, he didn't need a transfusion to flush the old culture out—but the rest of the company did. Unfortunately, Armstrong forgot that blood is transfused drip by drip, not all in a flood.

But wait—hasn't this book taught that dotcom speed leadership *cannot* be drip by drip? Shouldn't we be praising Mike Armstrong for taking an AT&T Solutions–style "bull by the horns" entrepreneurial approach?

In fact, we do praise Armstrong's decisive and courageous support of AT&T Solutions and his intention to quicken and embolden corporate AT&T's step. "Mike wanted to make AT&T much, much bigger and much, much more successful, not just inch along," AT&T Solutions CTO Dick Anderson said earlier in this book. "I think he already recognized that AT&T Solutions—with its small size, its proactive model, and its nimbleness—spurred growth."

The high-speed culture of AT&T Solutions naturally appealed to Armstrong, who, by both personal and professional nature, was a fast-lane driver himself.

"I believe what Armstrong appreciates most about AT&T Solutions is that we don't acknowledge constraints," Dick Anderson said.

AT&T Solutions, however, was a breakaway culture that could invent itself as it went along and was inherently light on its feet. In contrast, AT&T itself was still slogging through its own bureaucratic mud. By abruptly leaping forward it risked falling on its face.

"If there's anything [AT&T] must be, it's customer-centric and market-focused," Mike Armstrong told AT&T Solutions.

Says AT&T Solutions President Brian Maloney today, "For Mike, the AT&T Solutions cultural model is still a model for the new AT&T. He's still dedicated to serving clients, flexing to meet their changing needs, and listening to their concerns and advice. Both AT&T and AT&T Solutions sell skills and service more than products, so both organizations are committed to continuous learning to sharpen their skills and insights. That kind of nimbleness is a shared cultural trait."

We agree. And we stand by our espousal of a damn-the-torpedoes leadership approach—but only when a culture is up to speed and battle-ready and its torpedoes are ready to be fired, not stuck in the torpedo bay.

To shift the metaphor to sports: The 100-meter sprinter, to avoid pulling a hamstring when she bolts from the blocks, takes sufficient time to warm up.

The Indy 500 driver, to avoid hitting the wall, determines how fast his car can safely go. That's called driving on the limit, or on the ragged edge. Just within the edge, or right on it, and the driver is likely to be a winner. Over it, he's sure to crash. Either way, he's driving at breakneck speed—but with a measure of prudence he won't break his neck.

Our final note on Mike Armstrong's cultural sensitivity is a ringing note of praise—for promoting acculturation not just in business but in the realm of humankind.

Armstrong laments:

America suffers from a digital divide, even though minority families have had strong growth in computer use and access to the Internet. Overall, African-American and Latino families are less than half as likely as white households to explore the Internet from home, school, or work. This is an opportunity gap that America has to close. It's hard to talk about economic justice when too many kids are entering the workforce without the computer skills and Internet knowledge they need. While no single company can close this gap, AT&T is committed to provide free cable service to schools in the communities we serve and free high-speed Internet access to schools and libraries in those communities. It is our objective to wire the learning institutions that are unwired, to enable high-speed access to the Internet for those schools and libraries without access, and to deliver Internet service to be used by those who are un-served.

> The communications revolution isn't just a revolution in tech-
> nology. It's a revolution in opportunities. So the more inclusive
> the communications revolution can be, the faster that revolution
> will deliver benefits to America.
>
> In the great wave of immigration at the end of the last cen-
> tury, immigrant children came to the public schools and learned
> English. That was their ticket to success in the new world. That
> was the basis of the social and economic mobility that many of
> their parents never got. As we enter the new millennium, in a
> sense we are all immigrants. We are arriving in a new world cre-
> ated by technology. We all have to learn the language of comput-
> ers and the Internet. At AT&T, we think we can help.

This combination of business savvy and enlightened cultural
concern—in the largest human sense—suggests that Armstrong will
ultimately guide his corporate culture to great success.

ALLIANCES

"Entrepreneurs almost always form alliances," Rick has said. "Alliances
are magic—they make you bigger and more powerful than you are."

Mike Armstrong sought to be bigger and more powerful less by
allying with cable companies than by buying them up. As Cisco's John
Chambers watched AT&T pack on weight, he knew that the failure
rate for corporate acquisitions in his own industry was over 75 percent. Chambers admired and trusted Mike Armstrong, though, and
even as AT&T struggled to make a success of its one-stop communications services shop, Chambers didn't fear for AT&T's success.
"They put themselves into a very good position with their acquisition
strategy," he said.

A good starting position, however, doesn't always ensure a winning
position in the end. "Big corporations always have the problem of getting the right resources organized in the best way," said Bank One's
John Skubik.

John Chambers knew from his own experience that every acquisition was another high hurdle in a long and challenging race. "We
acquired over 61 companies," he said. "We had to rewrite the textbooks
about acquiring, and acquiring was every bit as difficult as we thought."

Compared to the 75 percent acquisition failure rate in its industry, Cisco did quite all right, though, scoring an 85 to 90 percent rate of success.

How did Cisco do it? The same way Chambers says any smart company can. "In the coming decade," he explains, "the companies who succeed will be those who know how to partner strategically. They'll be the ones who win."

Notice that Chambers says "partner" instead of "acquire." In his view, an acquisition must not be simply a purchase but should be a mutually profitable association of two parties who have established a professional and personal rapport.

The partnership must be *strategic* as well.

What strategy does Chambers suggest?

"Leading companies will be those that develop internally, acquire effectively, and form ecosystem partnerships in a horizontal business model," he states.

A *horizontal* business model—was this the kind of model Mike Armstrong initially designed and sought to create?

Yes, but his bundled services shop was an integrated *vertical* corporate structure, and a huge one at that.

For a CEO who "wanted to make AT&T much, much bigger and much, much more successful, not just inch along," the vertical model was obviously impossible to resist. The irony—even the paradox—was that while Armstrong was amassing and consolidating corporate power, he was acknowledging that the smaller, more proactive, nimbler AT&T Solutions model spurred growth.

"The more power you give away, the more powerful you will become" was the new economy's most instructive paradox for Rick.

We noted earlier that when AT&T Solutions was in its infancy, more and more big firms were doing spin-offs, carve-outs, sell-offs, and privatizations—breaking up and restructuring their assets to focus on their core competencies. Vertical integration was occurring downstream around competencies that brought companies closer to their customers, not farther away. Upstream processes were being "deverticalized"—or "horizontalized," you could say—and financially draining activities were facing elimination for economy's sake.

Says John Chambers, "Unlike a vertical business model in which a single company attempts to excel in every aspect of the business, the horizontal model allows multiple companies to combine their expertise to create comprehensive solutions for their customers."

This was a lesson that Mike Armstrong learned two years too late— or right on time, if you take on faith Armstrong's assertion that the breakup was a logical, predestined next step.

Of course, hard lessons are usually learned from hard experience. In this regard, Mike Armstrong ultimately proved himself strong, honest, and smart enough to read and respond to the writing on the wall.

QUINTESSENTIAL TEAMS

Since this book is primarily about AT&T Solutions—whose teams and teamwork we addressed in Chapter 7—we won't be assessing the internal teams of corporate AT&T. Instead, we will briefly regard AT&T as an overall team—quintessential or not—in itself. In fact, Mike Armstrong has viewed AT&T as just that: an assemblage of prime-time players all driven to work together in common cause.

As leader of this championship team, Armstrong is self-admittedly hands-on. "I spend a lot of time communicating to the company's employees and management," he has said. "I can't touch 150,000 people personally, but through the system I can. . . . I don't believe that you can lead unless you are involved and know what's going on and thus can appreciate the organization's problems, challenges, and demands. I know I'm sometimes criticized for being too hands-on, but unless I'm fully involved I can't support our people as I should."

According to Glenn Swift, Armstrong doesn't just push and prod his players; he inspires them with missionary zeal. Swift continued, "Mike Armstrong . . . says, what is our role, just transmitting electrons across a set of wires? No, anyone can do that. Our mission is using our talent, drive, and financial capacity to unleash value. That's what AT&T and AT&T Solutions are really all about."

AT&T Solutions' team spirit has inspired Armstrong, as Dick Anderson attests: "I think Mike has recognized that AT&T Solutions' bold ambitions, our devotion to teamwork, our reward system, and the way we focus on very clear growth targets should be emulated across AT&T."

In this book we've declared that AT&T Solutions exemplifies the quintessential organizational team, specifically in its rapid adaptivity, its inclusive embrace of customers, partners, and competitors along with its own employees, and in being geared to run at the speed of change. A critical element of this process is a proactive 360-degree feedback system that allows individuals to receive input from multiple sources in order to create customized personal development plans. Without this versatile team-building mechanism, employees fall into the trap of solely receiving top-down annual feedback designed to evaluate past results and to promote a poorly structured course to a future success.

Has Mike Armstrong made AT&T a quintessential team in these three regards?

His initial series of acquisitions certainly was an inclusive embrace of new partners—though the "partners" were not real allies in John Chambers' horizontal and ecosystematic sense of the word.

The current split-up of AT&T links the four new business units and their respective customers in a truer and far more promising alliance. Though operationally independent, each enterprise should be able to work "across space, time, and organizational boundaries with links strengthened by webs of technology," as Lipnack and Stamps say quintessential teams should.[2] As freestanding, cross-fertilizing units, the companies can now adapt to changing circumstances far more quickly than the bundled, bulked-up corporation ever could. With their gearshifts detached from the corporate transmission, they can push the stick into overdrive and cruise at high speed.

That's Mike Armstrong's hope and expectation—and ours, too.

PREDICTABLE PROBLEMS/FAILING FORWARD FAST

In his quest to create a network of bundled communications services, Mike Armstrong encountered acquisition approval delays, consumer indifference, software supply slowdowns, and a precipitous drop in the long-distance revenues that were supposed to keep the corporate ship afloat. All of these problems caused investors' patience to run out.

Were these problems predictable? Yes, they were. But the accelerating decline of long-distance was missed by the industry, the analysts, and the capital markets, as well as by AT&T.

Were they, in fact, predicted? We don't know if they were or were not—but if they were, their consequences were minimized or ignored, as the network bundled services strategy went through its scaling challenges.

We are now left to ask: Did the strategy fail forward or backward?

Was the failure fast enough to allow the captain time to right the ship before it foundered and sank?

As to the latter question—yes, the ship did founder, and yes, the captain did have time to change course and prevent the ship from sinking—at least for now.

Whether the failure was forward or backward depends on whether the liberated AT&T companies ultimately yield sweet or bitter fruit. Meanwhile, we can say that predicting the problems could have headed them off and thereby prevented the eventual failure, or minimized it at least.

But was the failure such a bad thing? Didn't John Chambers say he learns more from failure than from success?

Yes, he did say that, but he didn't say he continues walking toward a failure that is staring him in the face. We can infer, therefore, that when Chambers is able to predict failure, he changes course. Nevertheless, shouldn't we applaud Mike Armstrong for risking the company's fortunes on a bold gamble he thought would pay off? The AT&T Solutions original team of 12 lived for the exciting risks and the chance for their hard work to produce gold.

They understood the difference between smart, calculated risks and reckless gambling. Their teaming was laced with exhaustive research and rigorous forecasting along with their wide-eyed dreams and heartfelt beliefs.

The team became intrepid mariners, and when they're caught in storms and their ships are swamped, they bail them out, reset the rigging, and sail on toward port.

Of course, the captain may or may not heed the warnings of his crew. There was a culture and a long string of AT&T executives who felt the bundled bill strategy, which began before Armstrong's arrival, was a winning gambit. Armstrong, in fact, never believed that bundling on a bill was a viable strategy. He thought it was a convenience. The value would be bundling on the networks, and he invested heavily to deliver on his belief.

The AT&T Solutions model was tried and true and is the logical approach to inspire the parent company on a high-flying journey into much needed blue sky success. A lesson learned too late perhaps. And yet, the wise adventurers always learn from bruising experiences. They are strengthened by the Dream, Believe, Dare, Do principles—the very ones that continue to guide the ever dynamic and forward-moving AT&T Solutions team.

Epilogue

SETTING: An auditorium stage, seen on a computer screen in a December 2000 Web-cast electronic town meeting. Seated on the stage are five men:

Mike Armstrong, Chief Executive Officer of AT&T
Rick Roscitt, President of AT&T Business Services
Frank Ianna, President of AT&T Network Services
Brian Maloney, President of AT&T Solutions
Bill O'Brien, Vice President of Marketing of AT&T Solutions

Brian: Rick, was it hard to give up day-to-day control of AT&T Solutions?

Rick: It was the right thing to do at the right time.

Brian: Why was that?

Rick: The baby had grown up, to adolescence at least. It was larger than I could manage efficiently and effectively anymore. I had to let it go.

Brian: What do you mean you couldn't manage it anymore?

Rick: In terms of knowing everybody, hiring all the new talent, being everywhere at once—AT&T Solutions was now just so big. I mean, Mom and Pop can run a mom-and-pop store, but if they want to go global, they've got to give up total control. The fact is, I'd been releasing control of AT&T Solutions for the last couple of years. I had to. I'd become afraid to go to the men's room in case somebody needed me while I was there. Hey, we all are replaced sooner or later.

Brian: You're a good goose, Rick.

Rick: We're a good V-formation.

Brian: It's our culture.

Rick: And the culture allows things to go forward when one person isn't writing out every instruction and inspecting every detail.

Brian: Though we do have a lot of explicit guidelines on developing business cases and who signs off on them and how they align with the budget and on and on and on.

Rick: But no management model can anticipate and predict everything that may happen, and guide us every step of the way. So much of it is just playing our way through, and it's our culture that helps us do that. Once the culture is in place and a leadership succession model is set, the original leader can get out of the way.

Brian: Are you anxious for your baby now that it's out of your hands?

Rick: Not with you as president. I see you transferring people out of management and into line engagements, reshuffling the deck, and realigning resources. That's healthy, that's good. Course corrections are necessary from time to time. To grow we have to adjust. You were one of the original 12 in that broom closet; don't you miss it?

Brian: It was lonely in there. And crowded, too.

Rick: And about the most exciting thing you ever experienced.

Brian: It was—it's true.

Rick: You can bet there are new groups of 12 hatching their own enterprises right now, right inside AT&T. Thanks to Mike Armstrong, the entrepreneurial spirit is alive and well in this corporation. These new mavericks are running fast and, if they're like we were, they're running scared, too.

Bill: What do you mean, "scared," Rick?

Rick: I kind of agree with Andy Grove, the ex-chairman of Intel. He said only the paranoid survive. He meant that every day you've got to worry about the world figuring out what you're doing and jumping all over you. We felt that way in AT&T Solutions' early days. We were terrified that other outsourcers would catch up. Every morning we thought, "Is this our last day?" To make sure it wasn't, we innovated and morphed and moved into new services as fast as we could. We heard the footsteps behind us, so we didn't dare stand still. We kept moving the ball ahead. And it wasn't irrational to do that, because in this new economy you've got to keep sharpening your edge. If you don't, you'll lose it very fast. At the same time, you don't want to be the victim of your own success, and you don't want to bog down because you're too big and fat. Whenever we felt a bit of bureaucracy creeping in—and we did from time to time—we quickly shook things up.

Bill: Some people are concerned that AT&T Solutions will lose the spirit and agility of a small company now that we've merged with the larger ABS.

Rick: Are you concerned about that?

Bill: I'm concerned that we keep our spirit and agility but rein in our mad passion a bit.

Rick: What do you mean?

Bill: When we began, it was our culture to work 80 to 90 hours a week. That was our bravado. It was necessary at the beginning, but I wonder if it still is. Last night I was in the office until 3 a.m., and we ate 12 pizzas. We got the work out but at what physical and emotional cost? I think we need to find a healthier balance. People can burn both ends for a year or two, but then they burn out.

Rick: It's tricky, isn't it, since people come to AT&T Solutions because it's a mix of the big stable company and the maverick entrepreneur.

Bill: Right, we want it to be both. We're energized by that mix. We're driven, but we don't want to be driven off the edge. We want to be proud of working overtime but not just so we can say, "I ate three pizzas all by myself."

Rick: Speaking of motivation, talk about compensation at ABS.

Bill: There again, we have to be careful. AT&T Solutions people are very conscious of being AT&T Solutions people, and of playing different AT&T Solutions roles through their careers, and of being compensated differently for each one. They wear their AT&T Solutions red badge of courage on their sleeves. They're proud that clients are buying their specific, personal AT&T Solutions expertise more than they're buying corporate AT&T. Therefore I think we mustn't homogenize our AT&T Solutions compensation system to fit across the board with ABS.

Brian: AT&T Solutions' customers buy our specific expertise, and they stick with us because we always listen to them and tell them the truth.

Frank: Which is a good policy in dealing with Wall Street, too, I might add. Even when you're taking hits.

Brian: Tell us about that, Frank. In particular, how can a company keep an honest balance between its long-term projections and Wall Street's classic short-term view?

Frank: First, you need to get investors to agree that your long-term strategy is okay. Then you set expectations for accomplishments along the way. And then, of course, you make sure you do what you've said you'll do. If you don't hit your marks, you'll be in trouble. If you do, you'll be okay—though you won't always be rewarded right away. Your stock may move sideways for many months and quarters even while you're saying to people, "Hey, we just doubled in a day!" It's tough.

Mike: The main thing, I agree, is to tell the truth. For example, if you're not going to make your third and fourth quarters' projected results, don't fudge the facts and hope you can fix things quickly enough to avoid a jolt. You can't. Don't say to yourselves, "Let's not make this a material event." Because it is material, it's a huge critical mass, so instead of hiding it or dribbling it away, revise your outlook instead. Be up front with your customers and shareholders because ultimately they'll know it if you're not. AT&T is always forthright, and we take our punishment for it. Some others do, too. EDS, for instance, changes their sales and revenue projection and the market takes 20 points off their stock. An analyst changes his assessment of Motorola and their stock goes down 18 points—$30 billion in market value!

Rick: Still, we get the most attention when our stock is down. World-Com's stock drops even lower than ours does, but we take all the heat in the press. But would I trade places with WorldCom? Not for a second. It doesn't even cross my mind. We're an icon in America, and I'm proud of that. When I'm shaving in the morning I've got on CNBC, and if there's not a story about AT&T I'm shocked.

Mike: As a result of being honest and decisive enough to change course, we do take heat. Does straight shooting mean shooting yourself in the foot? No, not in the long run; there's just a short-term loss of blood. And Rick's right, each of us probably thinks we're getting the worst of it, but we're all getting hit. Misery loves company. Honesty does, too.

Brian: Was the decline of AT&T's stock what you would call "misery"?

Mike: No. And I'm being honest about that. It was sobering and disappointing of course, but mostly it was energizing because it put everything in sharp relief and made clear what we had to do next.

Rick: The breakup caused some concern among employees and customers of ABS. We're helping everyone understand the strategy, though, and people are feeling better as they see that ABS will now be more focused on giving clients what they want. Just as AT&T Solutions was always self-determining, now ABS will be, too.

Bill: How do you react to the press saying that Mike has completely abandoned his strategy to make AT&T a one-stop communications services shop?

Rick: I think the press is incorrect. ABS, for example, will be bundling other AT&T divisions' services into what we sell—not because

AT&T Corporation says we must, but because our customers want us to. We've already struck a deal with AT&T Wireless to represent all their products, and we'll have a similar deal with AT&T Cable. We'll also be doing business with outside companies, so we're really freer and looser than before to act in our own and our customers' best interests. It's the same way that AT&T Solutions has always worked.

Brian: At AT&T Solutions I'm excited, not worried, about the restructuring. Sure, we watch the stock price for what it means to our personal wealth and our market reputation, but it doesn't change the fundamental way we do business. We've still got to execute, we've still got to grow. And our culture isn't changed; it's still about serving our customers, flexing to meet their changing needs, celebrating our successes, admitting our mistakes, continually educating and reeducating ourselves, and putting people—ourselves and our clients—first.

Rick: Culture is the key to success. And much as I admire Mike, and much as I'd like to pat myself on my own back for being a strong leader, I don't believe culture depends on the person at the top. By that I mean culture must be disseminated and reinforced—over and over and over—until it is absorbed throughout the ranks. That way you end up with a culture of people, not personality.

Brian: Exactly. Rick has done a fabulous job with AT&T Solutions, but it's not the Rick Roscitt Show. It's the AT&T Solutions show, the AT&T Solutions culture, and it's permeating AT&T Business Services now, just as it's inspiring all of AT&T. It's being institutionalized in a wider and wider way, rooting deeper and getting stronger so it can sustain itself over the long haul.

Rick: Yes, it's essential to take the long-haul view, not just of AT&T Solutions and ABS, but also of all of AT&T's new component parts. The business world is so volatile, so fickle, and so harsh. Assessments are based on short-term results that are not indicative of true value. In snapshots, the economy is unfathomable. In fiscal-year stints, it's hard to predict. But over 30-year periods it makes wavelike sense. Look at the Internet phenomenon: the initial boom ended, but the layoffs and company closings will end, too.

Brian: For the present, Frank, how do you think the dotcom failures will affect the e-business phenomenon? Will some companies step back a bit and be a little more cautious?

Frank: I believe we're still in the blossoming stage, with some new seedlings still not yet popped up. This'll most likely continue for the next year or two. Eventually, one-third of the dotcoms will succeed, one-third will fail, and one-third will be bought up. And then the industry will consolidate.

Bill: I don't think there's any question that some of these dotcoms are going to find themselves in very deep trouble as the stock market takes these huge capitalizations. And this will drive consolidation. And so once again in a free market economy, the strong and fit will survive. We just hope too many customers don't get hurt and that those who do aren't disenchanted with networking technology as a result. But that isn't likely to happen, because the technology is too pervasive, and the survivors will take up the slack and learn from the losers' mistakes.

Rick: The Internet is still blossoming, I agree. It's got such a cache. Just to be online is the thing, let alone what you'll do there. Lou Gerstner wrote a few weeks ago about some big clients' CEOs saying, "Let's do something on the Net. Anything." So they can say they're there, so they can feel better. They'd never have said that 10 years ago. Now to get their attention we ask them, "Are you online now? What's your Net strategy? Are you trading 24 hours a day?" They perk up.

Brian: Yes, I'm surprised by how many clients go online for no good reason. They're just afraid of being scooped. Our job is to help them be smart about e-business, to understand not just how but also why they should go online, so they get the best results.

Frank: Again, so many want to be Amazon.com.

Rick: Which hasn't turned a profit yet! But survivability aside, Amazon's a great example of both high tech and high touch.

Brian: Explain that, Rick.

Rick: Having just the tech or just the touch won't cut it anymore; you can't survive without them both. You sign on to Amazon, they know who you are right away. They know the last book you bought, they know what else you enjoy reading, and so they can offer you choices you'll probably like. They're using their real-time high-tech database and their 24-hour interactive networking capability to transform the shopping experience. They're making it more intimate, and they're getting closer in touch with you. Whereas at a brick-and-mortar Barnes and Noble store, unless you give the clerk your name and biography, you're just an anonymous face. Though B and N sells a fine cappuccino, I'll say that.

Brian: Barnes and Noble is getting higher-tech and higher-touch now, too.

Rick: Which proves my point. But Amazon was first, so they're perceived as being the high-tech, high-touch number one. They've blended the best of both worlds.

Mike: In fact, the most likely outcome for most retail businesses is a hybrid model. It's already heading that way. In the 1999 holiday season, for example, brands with both physical and Internet sites sold better than brands selling only online.

Brian: So the Internet won't kill Main Street.

Mike: No, clicks won't knock down all the bricks. But Main Street will be forced to be more nimble because people want more and more options and faster response. And since the barriers to entering the Internet are so low, even small retailers can use the Internet to sell goods, and that means more jobs all around.

Frank: Bill, with AT&T blending its illustrious history as a telecommunications provider and its newer face as a networking services specialist—creating its own high-tech and high-touch, so to speak—what's your biggest future challenge from a marketing point of view?

Bill: Continuing to have the most compelling value proposition in IT networking and telling the world loudly and clearly enough that we do.

Frank: Are we loud and clear enough now?

Bill: We're still at risk of other companies positioning us as just a components supplier, even after all the networking engagements we've done. If AT&T isn't also seen as strong in IT systems integration, then it'll still be dependent on long-distance cents-per-minute, which is a commodity now. And pretty soon our commodity position will be zero because of smaller companies pitching cheaper long-distance capability alone—the Bell companies, for instance, and Sprint and MCI. Many people at AT&T think MCI WorldCom is the devil incarnate. I think MCI is just like us. They're tearing their hair out right this minute about these same issues from their side of the fence.

Frank: Qwest and Frontier will also be competing in long-distance when the artificial regulations go away.

Bill: That'll be even more voice traffic capacity, with the prices coming down from 50 cents a minute once upon a time to 6, 5, or 4! I don't want to build my business on that. I wouldn't stake my 401(k) on long-distance, you know? We've got to live or die on our proven ability to provide networking business solutions.

Frank: While half a dozen or more other companies are doing networking, too.

Bill: And most of them aren't half our size! Because the entry threshold is so low, it's just intellectual capacity and ability—and being credible with customers. Well, AT&T Solutions can't just be credible with customers; we've got to be the gold standard. We've got to be their first choice.

Brian: Regarding the smaller long-distance providers, Rick, will we ever see AT&T merging with a "Baby Bell"?

Rick: I don't know if it's possible from a regulatory standpoint, but in the past the FCC didn't like the idea. It seems inevitable that we'll see further consolidation in the telecommunications industry, and then a handful of global players will do everything from local to long-distance to global, and from satellite to terrestrial to fixed wireless and mobile wireless. The silicon chip will be embedded in everything, from soda machines to kiosks in airports and malls, making almost all devices digital communicators. The ability to connect anything digital to anything else digital on a nonstop, real-time basis is here today. If we take out the regulatory and geographic borders that have been somewhat artificially set up and allow this technology to be expansively deployed by large worldwide organizations and used by everyone from mom-and-pop stores to huge corporations, we're going to see a different world in this new millennium. I don't think the regulatory processes, well intentioned as they are, can do much more than slow this down. They're not going to stop this trend because it's too forceful, it's too overwhelming, and it's too real.

Mike: Looking at both the huge corporations and the mom-and-pops, we've learned that it's the fast—not just the big—who prevail. Fast doesn't just mean having a quick idea, or rolling out a new dotcom, or remaking your vision overnight. It means redefining and transforming your company at the moment you need to and not waiting until it's too late. It means executing your vision with efficiency and precision and thereby meeting your commitments without fail. Speed of this kind determines which dotcoms become real companies and which real companies evolve and prosper at the speed of change.

Brian: Overall, Mike, does regulation help or hurt this evolution?

Mike: Let's jump ahead a hundred years and ask two questions. One, during the twenty-first century, did communications technology improve the lives of people around the world? That's easy. The answer will be "yes." Question two is, Were people's lives improved quickly and efficiently because industry regulators did all they could to accelerate progress, or did the regulators enforce the outdated twentieth-century regulatory model and thus hold things up?

Brian: Can't the industry and the regulators work together?

Mike: They can and they must. They have a joint responsibility to keep the flywheel of competition and technology turning. But the focus of regulation must change. The days of preserving artificial markets through regulatory restrictions have to end. The regulator's job is protecting the public interest while letting market forces work. The faster the flywheel of competition turns, the faster the public receives the benefits.

Brian: Don't burgeoning Internet services today show that the flywheel sometimes turns too fast for regulators to keep pace?

Mike: Yes, and in this situation the marketplace is governing itself faster and more efficiently than any government agency ever could.

Brian: How should the government protect the public interest while letting market forces work?

Mike: First, by preserving, protecting, and promoting competition. Second, by encouraging self-regulation and self-policing by the Internet industry on a global scale. The Internet is a global medium and we don't want a patchwork of national regulations without any consistency. The government can help us avoid that. We need non-restrictive global standards very quickly, and regulators should be focusing on that. The International Telecommunications Union was founded in 1865 to set standards for interconnection and operation of telegraph service. Since then it's done a great job of negotiating interconnection standards from a variety of national standards. But the standard-setting approach that worked in the nineteenth and twentieth centuries can't do the job in the twenty-first. The pace is just too fast. A new service can be obsolete by the time standards are set. We need true global standards, deployed quickly and cooperatively by the industry and the ITU. The alternative is a series of competing proprietary standards. And that alternative is lurking right around the bend.

Brian: AT&T Solutions is an enterprise spun off by the flywheel of competition and technology. What aspects of the AT&T Solutions culture have permeated and inspired the rest of AT&T?

Mike: Certainly, the entrepreneurial drive. And the courage to take risks. And the willingness to make 5- and 10-year contractual commitments, with strict P&L accountability right down to the account level. We want to see AT&T behaving like that, all the new divisions, right across the board.

Rick: I see citizens behaving like that, taking risks, embracing change, the older and younger generations alike. Look at these men and women in their eighties with their laptops, checking their stock portfolios, trading online. Just a few years ago a lot of people shied away from the Internet, saying it was too strange, too hard to understand and describe. Now we're all logged on. So our society runs with the tide, but will businesses keep up? Sure, they dream about being Amazon.com, but will they dare to become full participants in the networking-centric age?

Brian: Give us an example of an industry that will be networking-centric a short distance down the road.

Rick: Auto parts. GM or Ford or Chrysler will need a million carburetors; they'll go online with their specifications and say who wants to build them, who wants to bid? Like an eBay for automotives. There's one of these already in the paper industry, and one in petrochemicals, and others are springing up. It takes the face-to-face brokers out of the game, and without middle people the business model is faster and more efficient. Companies that don't change to networking-centric models and who stick with their physical operations will be in trouble. They won't lead at the speed of change. They won't extend their reach. They won't go global at the speed of light, they'll just putter around at home.

Frank: I was in Mexico in '97 being interviewed in Spanish by CNN. The questions were translated into English, then my answers were put into Spanish so the viewers would know what I said. The first question was, "Does AT&T see the Internet as a threat?" I responded that some people see it as a threat but AT&T sees it as a great opportunity. "Who's threatened?" the interviewer asked me. "Businesses that move most of their information in physical form," I said, "and who think their physical processes are far advanced enough."

I was asked to be more specific, so I told a story. I said I used to waste two Saturday mornings a month paying bills. While I did, I thought about how AT&T did billing, which was an amazing enterprise in itself.

We started with huge rolls of paper; then the computer printed the statements, collated them, stuffed them in envelopes, zip-coded and bar-coded them, sorted them in trays, and wrapped them all up for mailing. Not a human hand in sight.

When payments came in, a machine measured the thickness of each envelope and sensed the four essential sheets—the front, the back, the remittance document, and the check. If there were additional sheets, the envelope was spit out for manual processing.

Otherwise, the machine zipped open the envelope, shredded it for recycling, took the check and the remittance document, flash-photographed both sides of each, read the remittance sheet's bar code to see how much was owed, optically scanned what the customer had written on the check, and compared this figure with the due amount. If it matched, the machine processed the check and automatically debited the customer's account.

Still no human intervention—unless the check's amount was wrong or unreadable and an error alert flashed on a screen. I once watched a lady monitoring these discrepancies. She handled 2200 of them per hour. She'd see an alert on the screen, enter it on a keyboard, and with her first stroke the next alert popped up. She kept going and going, doing each one in just a little over a second. It was breathtaking.

Well, I said to the interviewer, the Internet wipes that whole process out. It eliminates the whole physical bill-paying infrastructure. And puts that lady out of work.

Now on Saturday morning I log on to AT&T, I check my bill, I verify that it's correct, I click in my payment, and it's done. No paper, no mail truck, no remittance-checking machine, no lady checking the screen.

That's killer IT application—it kills whatever system was being used before. And it's lethal to companies that can't or won't adopt the new IT technologies. Of course, most of them aren't IT experts, so they need solutions from outsourcing specialists like AT&T Solutions. That's our sweet spot in this industry, and it's getting sweeter as we speak.

Mike: Jeff Bezos of Amazon said this about e-business being a threat: "We on the Internet should be terrified of customers because they are loyal to us right up to the point that someone else offers a better service. The power shifts to the consumer online." So our challenge is focusing more than ever on customer needs—being customer-intimate, if you will. This means shifting from competition on price to competition on quality and service, which is a positive development, I believe. So how do we compete and win in these customer-intimate arenas? By mastering the technology as it roars ahead. By energizing our vision, intellect, and attitudes to run at the speed of change. This applies not just to individual businesses, but also to America as a whole. Our national culture is creative and innovative, we've always nurtured and embraced new technologies. They drive our market system. They're the real gold backing up our currency. They maintain our leadership position in the world.

Brian: We're leaders, but the Internet is also giving other countries opportunities to forge ahead. It's democratizing commerce.

Mike: This Internet phenomenon is an extraordinary event. It's changing the way we network and it's also transforming social and political structures around the world. It's global regardless of the system of government. It's a forum not just for commerce but also for ideas and opinions of every sort.

Brian: As technology roars ahead, what's in the pipeline, Frank?

Frank: In a word, broadband. Not just for business but in the home. And not just local service; it'll be packetized broadband connections to all-distance networks for data, video, and voice. It'll replicate the local service you used to have from the Bell operating company: pick up and get a dial tone.

Mike: Yes, narrowband is a thing of the past. We've made that twisted copper wire go just as fast as it can. I remember selling a 4800-baud modem and thinking that was the living end. Now it's end-to-end broadband as we drive those light waves over those fibers at an ever-increasing rate. Soon the old smokestacks that drove video over coaxial cable, voice over twisted wire, computer data through the modem, will be gone, made obsolete. The new technology will bring a convergence of information, communications, and entertainment. Your cable link will not only deliver hundreds of channels, it'll make a virtual communications center out of your TV.

Frank: An example of that right now is full-motion video on the Internet. If you're house hunting in San Diego you can click on a house, go inside, send the camera room to room. You want to buy an Explorer? Here, watch a video clip, check out the interior, look at the dashboard, and go for a ride! The bandwidth permits so much information and graphics, and it's speeding up PCs.

Brian: Reality is catching up with innovation.

Frank: The technology is catching up with the need.

Rick: We're listening to our customers, so the innovation never stops.

Mike: I was involved in managing the introduction of the IBM personal computer. The marketplace was skeptical back then. People said, Why do we need a 16-bit machine? Isn't 8 bits enough? Put an operating system on our desks? You gotta be crazy! Now customers have a nearly insatiable need for speed. They're frustrated that 280 million hours are wasted every year simply waiting for files to download. With broadband, our industry is increasing the speed and capacity of our networks. We're installing broadband cable systems with the capacity to transmit 150 years of *The New York Times* over a single fiber in a single second. And these systems are growing at a breakneck rate: 2800 miles of fiber cable are being installed every hour somewhere in the world, enough to circle the globe twice every 24 hours. Simultaneously, we're in the midst of a wireless revolution. Within three years there will be a wireless phone for every six people on earth—a billion wireless phones throughout the world. By 2003, there will be twice as many wireless phones as there are homes with personal computers.

Brian: Time flies when we're having fun.

Mike: It took radio 30 years to reach its first 50 million people. It took TV just 13 years to do the same. It took the World Wide Web half as much time to reach twice as many people: 100 million people today surf the Internet. I suspect our grandchildren will think it was quaint of us to stick that black phone receiver against our ear and just speak and listen. Or to sit in front of that box and just watch.

Frank: Speaking of our progeny, my daughters are 22 and 11, my son's 15; they're all Internet-centric. They don't pull out the encyclopedia, they go to *Encyclopedia Britannica* online. I work for AT&T, but when I want to fix my computer I ask my son. In fact, I can barely type, I do about 15 words a minute. My e-mails are very short: "Yes. No. Give me a call, we'll talk."

Rick: Young people are major Internet consumers. Which means they're charging their purchases, of course.

Frank: My son surprised me the other day; he asked me for help on his machine. I told him sure, I'll try. He said, "Well, I don't really need help, I just need your credit card." And I said, "Rob, hand me that little mirror on the shelf, okay?" He said, "What do you need it for?" I answered, "So I can see if I look dumb." "So I'm not getting the credit card, right?" he said. And I said, "Yup, that's right."

Rick: Many people use credit cards casually today, but at the same time there's concern about the security of giving card numbers over the Net.

Frank: My father's an example of that. He won't give his credit card number over the phone. He asked me the other day, "How do I get an airline ticket?" I said, "Call up Continental and give the agent your card number." He said, "I'm not going to do that, it's unsafe." I said, "Dad, when you charge your dinner in a restaurant, what do they do with your credit card?" He said, "They take it in the back." I said, "Well, isn't that unsafe, too?" He said no, it wasn't. I asked him why not, and he said, "I don't know."

Brian: Rick, you brought up young people using the Internet. When young people ask you what it takes to be successful in today's computer-centric world, what do you say?

Rick: First of all, I tell them that I'm an overnight success—it just took me 27 years to become one. As for what it takes to be successful, I think the young people are looking for tricks of the trade, and I only have one. I tell them the reason I'm successful is I enjoy what I do. When you love your job and you're willing to work hard at it, you just need average intelligence to achieve what you want. Take a dream, believe in it, dare to pursue it, and then do what it takes to make it come true. The trick is loving every minute.

And I still do.

Afterword

Breaking the speed limits is critical to leading at the speed of change. And knowing one's limits and when to leave is critical to the effectiveness of a great leader. During most of Rick Roscitt's career at AT&T, he was the consummate maverick and rebel. He reinvented products, created new markets, and regained lost customers. Spending the next four years in the executive offices working on a traditional breakup strategy would have been pure torture for Rick. He knew that it was time to embark upon a fresh challenge.

Approximately six weeks prior to the release of this book, Rick Roscitt became the chairman and CEO of ADC Telecommunications Inc. The company makes systems that crank up the rate at which voice, data, and video signals are transmitted. We believe that Rick's outstanding leadership talents and success model will accelerate ADC to great heights.

Yet Rick's legacy lives on at AT&T Solutions. With a visionary new president, Brian Maloney, and a totally dedicated staff of over 12,000 strong, AT&T Solutions continues to lead at the speed of change.

Notes

Preface

1. *Walt Disney's Famous Quotes*, The Walt Disney Company, 1994.

Chapter 1

1. Rick Roscitt, "Value-Driven Networking: Planning for Success in the New E-conomy," PowerPoint Presentation, August 1999.
2. "How to Outsource for Competitive Advantage," *Forbes*, 10/20/97, paid advertising section.
3. Ibid.
4. Roscitt.
5. Roscitt.
6. Roscitt.
7. Roscitt.

Chapter 2

1. Rick Roscitt, "Value-Driven Networking: Planning for Success in the New E-conomy," PowerPoint Presentation, August 1999.
2. Ibid.

Chapter 3

1. "Outsourcing 2000," *Leaders*, Vol. 23, no. 1.

Chapter 4

1. Matt Krantz, "Unit of AT&T Reaps Rewards in Short Order," *Investor's Business Daily*, 3/31/98.
2. "AT&T Now Offers Full Service," *Information Week*, 2/27/95.
3. John J. Keller, "AT&T Sets Up Unit to Manage Computer Network for Clients," *The Wall Street Journal*, 2/15/95.
4. "Strategic Advantage through Intelligent Networking," special advertising section, AT&T Solutions.
5. "How to Outsource for Competitive Advantage," *Forbes*, 10/20/97, paid advertising section.
6. Rick Roscitt, "Value-Driven Networking: Planning for Success in the New E-conomy," PowerPoint Presentation, August 1999.
7. "Strategic Advantage through Intelligent Networking."
8. Seth Schiesel, "The No. 1 Customer: Sorry, It Isn't You," *The New York Times*, 11/23/97.
9. Tom Avril, "AT&T Unit Finds the Right Solution," *The Star-Ledger*, 12/31/97.

Chapter 5

1. "AT&T Names Roscitt President and CEO of Consulting Unit," *The Wall Street Journal*, 8/14/97.
2. Tom Avril, "Emerging AT&T Unit Gets New Leader," *The Star-Ledger*, 8/14/97.
3. Rebecca Quick, "AT&T's Solutions Will Run Parent's Computer Network," *The Wall Street Journal*, 9/10/97.
4. Bruce Caldwell, "AT&T Outsources to AT&T," *Information Week*, 9/15/97.
5. Mark Mehler, "AT&T Solutions Takes Over Parent Company's MIS Operations," *Integration Management*, 9/18/97.
6. Rebecca Blumenstein and Raju Narisetti, "AT&T to Pay $5 Billion for IBM Network," *The Wall Street Journal*, 12/9/98.

Chapter 6

1. Rebecca Blumenstein and Raju Narisetti, "AT&T to Pay $5 Billion for IBM Network," *The Wall Street Journal*, 12/9/98.
2. "Outsourcing for Business Transformation," *Fortune*, 6/7/99, paid advertisement.

Chapter 7

1. "Outsourcing 2000," *Leaders*, Vol. 23, no.1.
2. "AT&T's Solution to the Technology Revolution," *Leaders*, July-August-September, 1998.
3. Jessica Lipnack and Jeffrey Stamps, *Virtual Teams: Reaching Across Space, Time, and Organizations with Technology*, John Wiley & Sons, 1997.

Chapter 9

1. "AT&T Wins Contract Worth About $60 Million a Year for 10 Years to Manage McDermott Global IT," AT&T press release, 3/31/99.
2. "Exodus, AT&T Solutions Collaborate for Merrill Lynch Online (MLOL)," AT&T press release, 10/18/99.
3. "Bank One Expands Technology One Alliance with AT&T and IBM: Awards Additional Contracts Totaling More Than $600 Million," AT&T press release, 8/11/99.
4. "AT&T Wins $1.1B Textron Contract," *New York Post*, 9/11/96.
5. "AT&T Wins Over $2 Billion in Contracts," *The Wall Street Journal*, 9/11/96.
6. Lane F. Cooper, "AT&T Solutions Gains Contract to Manage McGraw-Hill Network," *Integration Management*, 3/16/98.
7. Mel Duvall, "AT&T, Citibank Sign Huge Contract," *Inter@ctive Week*, 3/16/98.
8. Alan Levinsohn, "Citibank Recharts Its Technology Course," *ABA Banking Journal*, 5/98.
9. Rick Roscitt, "Value-Driven Networking: Planning for Success in the New E-conomy," PowerPoint Presentation, August 1999.
10. "AT&T Solutions Helps Citibank Deploy Its Integrated Global Data Network," *Fortune*, 7/20/98, paid advertising section.

Chapter 10

1. Mike Armstrong, "The Internet and E-commerce," speech delivered to White Paper for Internet Policy Institute, 3/28/00.
2. "Halla Chooses AT&T Solutions Again," AT&T press release, 3/11/97.
3. Mike Armstrong, "Networking: The New Generation Comes of Age," speech delivered to ComNet/DC '99, 1/26/99.
4. Rebecca Blumenstein and Raju Narisetti, "AT&T to Pay $5 Billion for IBM Network," *The Wall Street Journal*, 12/9/98.
5. "AT&T's Solution to the Technology Revolution," *Leaders*, July-August-September 1998.
6. "Outsourcing 2000," *Leaders*, Vol. 23, no. 1.
7. "Outsourcing for Business Transformation," *Fortune*, paid advertisement section, 6/7/99.

Chapter 11

1. James W. Michaels, "Alan Greenspan Comes to the Party," *Forbes*, 7/17/00.
2. Jay Akasie, "Ford's Model E," *Forbes*, 7/17/00.

Chapter 12

1. "AT&T's Solution to the Technology Revolution," *Leaders*, July-August-September 1998.
2. Jessica Lipnack and Jeffrey Stamps, *Virtual Teams: Reaching Across Space, Time, and Organizations with Technology*, John Wiley & Sons, 1997.

Index

About the Authors

BILL CAPODAGLI and LYNN JACKSON are the founders of Capodagli Jackson Consulting, an Indianapolis-based firm that partners with Fortune 500 as well as entrepreneurial companies to help them transform corporate cultures, improve customer service, and increase market share. Based on Walt Disney's Dream, Believe, Dare, Do principles, their famous *Dream*ovations strategic planning approach continues to breathe new life into companies across industry lines. Drawing on their nearly half century of combined consulting experience, Capodagli and Jackson are popular seminar and keynote presenters around the world and frequent contributors to professional training and management journals. They co-wrote the best-selling management manifestos *The Disney Way* and *The Disney Way Fieldbook*. Bill and Lynn may be reached at Capodagli Jackson Consulting in Indianapolis; capojac@aol.com; 800-238-9958.